THE BIG
PAYOFF

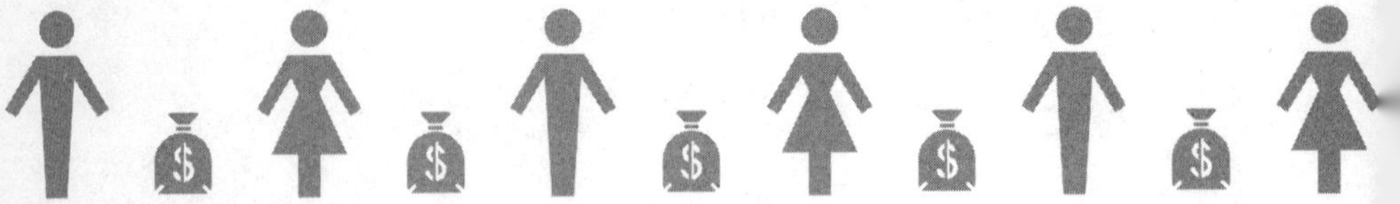

THE BIG PAYOFF

*8 Steps Couples Can Take to
Make the Most of Their Money—
and Live Richly Ever After*

Sharon Epperson

Collins

An Imprint of HarperCollinsPublishers

The names and identifying characteristics of parents and children featured throughout this book have been changed to protect their privacy. Any resemblance to actual persons, living or dead, is purely coincidental.

The information in this book has been carefully researched, and all efforts have been made to ensure accuracy. While the investment advice described in this book is believed to be effective there is no guarantee that it will benefit you in specific applications, owing to the risk that is involved in investing of almost any kind. Thus, neither the publisher nor the author assume liability for any losses that may be sustained by the use of the advice described in this book, and any such liability is hereby expressly disclaimed.

HarperCollins books may be purchased for educational, business, or sales promotional use. For information please write: Special Markets Department, HarperCollins Publishers, 10 East 53rd Street, New York, NY 10022.

FIRST EDITION

Designed by Nicola Ferguson

Library of Congress Cataloging-in-Publication Data

Epperson, Sharon.
The big payoff: 8 steps couples can take to make the most
of their money—and live richly ever after / by Sharon Epperson.—1st ed.
p. cm.
Includes index.
ISBN: 978-0-06-074488-5
ISBN-10: 0-06-074488-X
1. Couples—Finance, Personal. 2. Financial security. I. Title.

HG179.E66 2007
332.024'01—dc22   2006051717

07 08 09 10 11 WBC/RRD 10 9 8 7 6 5 4 3 2 1

For Dylan and Emma

CONTENTS

ACKNOWLEDGMENTS

As a television correspondent for more than 10 years, I'm accustomed to working with a talented team of reporters, producers, photographers, and editors. While some authors may view writing a book as a solitary endeavor, I approached researching, reporting, and writing *The Big Payoff* as I would any big story, drawing on the expertise of financial advisers and analysts, the experiences of many couples, and lots of encouragement from friends and colleagues. There are many people I must thank.

Several years ago, HarperCollins CEO Jane Friedman offered me insights into her own tremendously successful career and shared her working mom wisdom. Meeting her inspired me to add author to my resume and pitch this book idea.

I'm thrilled to have worked with Kathyrn Huck, a very patient and understanding editor, who gave me the extra time I needed on my first book.

My literary agent Caron Knauer was incredibly supportive of this idea from the beginning and my talent rep Larry Kramer is always in my corner offering encouraging words as I try to figure out how to juggle my on-air work and other writing projects.

CNBC president Mark Hoffman and senior vice president Jonathan Wald have created a work environment where good writing—for television, print, and online—is nurtured and praised. Thank you. I owe a special thanks to CNBC managing editor Tyler Mathisen for reading the manuscript and encouraging me to "boil it down" to bring out the best parts.

Jon Newman of Newman & Associates, a conscientious financial adviser, has been a great guide for me and my husband as we embark on our own quest to achieve the "big payoff." I appreciate your insights.

Michelle Massie assisted me with some of the initial interviews for this book. Tara Harper and Lisa Bryan had terrific comments on the manuscript. John Edwards offered helpful suggestions on the final draft as did Terri Hyacinth and Dean Rinella. Without Bibi Ally, I doubt I could have found the time to buckle down and write. And thanks to Lynne Robinson Phillips for listening and letting me know I could get it done!

I also owe tremendous thanks to experts who assisted in my research and/or read chapters and offered comments: Denise Appleby of Appleby Retirement Consulting, Patricia Brennan of Key Financial, David Cannon of Kaufmann Feiner, Lawrence Chane of Blank Rome, Dr. Charles Cutler of Aetna, Mark Foreman of the Connecticut Association of Realtors, Ruth Gastel and Steven Weisbart of the Insurance Information Institute, Joe Hurley of *SavingforCollege.com*, Ivory Johnson of the Scarborough Group, Benjamin Lewis of Perception, Greg McBride of *Bankrate.com*, and Sue Nester and Bob Rusbuldt of the Independent Insurance Agents and Brokers of America.

I certainly could not have written this book without the constant support and encouragement of a fantastic family. Thanks to Ena and Rawle Farley. Mom, Dad, Ben, and Lia, you are *always* there for me. I love you!

Finally, I owe the deepest and most sincere thanks to my muse, my soul mate, my husband, Chris, and our two wonderful children.

INTRODUCTION
The Path to the Payoff—Start Now. Start Talking. It's Never Too Late.

The first time we met with our financial adviser, my husband, Chris, did something I never would have expected.

But more on that in a minute.

My husband and I didn't sit down and prioritize our financial goals as a couple until several years after our wedding. We spent the first few years of our marriage, well, spending. We took trips to Ireland, Brazil and Japan; we saw plays, movies, concerts; we ate at some of the best restaurants in New York. But when we decided it was time to move out of our Manhattan apartment, find a house and have kids, we also agreed it was time to get serious about our finances.

I thought getting a financial adviser would be the first thing to do. I was very excited about the meeting. My husband was not. I thought we had a pretty good handle on our finances, and I wanted verification that we were on the right track. My husband viewed our first financial planning session as cheerfully as you might regard dental surgery (without novocaine).

During our meeting, Chris kept his remarks brief, while I tended to give long, detailed responses to the adviser's questions about our spending and saving habits. Chris's remarks were as abbreviated as a movie trailer; mine were like the director's cut DVD of *Titanic*. But it was all good—I thought the session was going well. Our adviser was very helpful in explaining everything we would need to develop a comprehensive financial plan. It was essential information. We talked about saving for retirement and our children's college expenses, establishing an emergency fund, and finding the right insurance policies.

It was during a detailed description of the difference between whole and term life insurance coverage that my husband did something supremely surprising.

He fell asleep.

I was extremely embarrassed that Chris did not seem to be interested in the money matters of our relationship. I had spent hours crunching numbers on retirement. I had spent long nights using mortgage calculators on the Internet. I had used weekends to compare insurance policies. What did it say about our marriage that I was more interested in our financial matters than he was? What impact would it have on our portfolio? On our relationship? On our future?

Finance is the enemy of romance. If you're thinking about money 24-7, chances are you're not thinking enough about your husband or your children. If you're constantly worrying about retirement or college savings, you may not be paying all the attention you should to soccer practice, or parent-teacher conferences, or "date night" dinners and movies or all the things that make life worth saving for.

Good financial planning isn't just about numbers on a computer screen. Good financial planning helps you get control of your money matters so you can stop fretting about cash and start focusing on your life. The same qualities that go into creating a lasting relationship—understanding, compromise, and patience—are also important when it comes to building a secure financial future.

It's tough enough to get a handle on money matters when you're single. Things get even more challenging when you're part of a couple. Smart financial decisions require a cool hand. But decisions made by a couple require a warm heart as well. How do you find a balance between the hand and the heart, between love and money?

Getting sound financial advice is the first step. People tell things to their financial advisers that they won't tell to their friends or family members. Have you ever told a friend how much money you make in salary? Probably not—but you might have confided to a close friend about how your hubby is doing in bed. Do you keep your mother up to date on your annual bonuses? Most likely no—but you might have filled mom in on your kid's potty training progress. Have you ever told a boyfriend or girlfriend your net worth? Of course not—but you may have spilled your guts about how a previous boyfriend or girlfriend made you feel worthless. Money is the last American taboo. People will talk about religion in public restrooms, they'll gab about sex in taxicabs, and they'll go into loud, echoing detail about ointment-requiring medical conditions on subway platforms. Nobody likes breathing a word about how much they make. We routinely act like we make much more, or much less, than we really do.

But the bigger, more important, secret is this: how to let go of our investment inhibitions. In divulging their finances, couples are forced to come to terms with their own fears and anxieties about managing debt while living comfortably, saving for retirement, and putting money away for their children's education. It's important to learn what most people have never been taught—how to talk about money with one's significant other in a way that's productive and profitable.

Having the background to make smart financial decisions and select suitable financial advisers has become even more important in the post-Enron-Tyco-WorldCom world. In an age when corporate chieftains routinely take perp walks, and when the starchiest of Wall Street firms and Main Street mutual fund companies have faced questions about honesty, you shouldn't leave your financial future in the hands of others without knowing exactly what you're doing.

Look in the mirror. Then look through this book. You are your first and best financial adviser. It's important to do your homework, even before you make the choice about whether or not to get professional financial advice. Average investors have become increasingly disenchanted with investment firms that profited on conflicts of interest between brokers and research analysts. Mutual fund holders and employees who contribute to 401(k) plans at work pulled millions of their hard-earned dollars from fund companies a few years ago following the revelation that fund managers at some firms engaged in shady trading practices. Now that new pension-reform legislation has made it easier for employers to offer 401(k) participants advice about their investments, it's even more important to do your own homework. Investigations into the insurance industry have forced consumers to pay closer attention to how agents and brokers are compensated. Your confidence in the so-called pros of the financial community is probably shaken. Whom do you trust? How can you trust anyone?

Finding trustworthy counsel is difficult. You almost don't want to trust people that seem too interested in the matter. Many couples are shy about seeking the help of a financial adviser and may feel uncomfortable sharing details with the adviser they end up choosing. When it comes to family finances, one thing is usually true: very soon, it's too late. Unfortunately for many couples, without a third party facilitating the conversation, serious discussions about finances may be put off for far too long. I know a couple with two teenage sons who still have not begun to save for college. Mounting money concerns played a role in this couple's eventual divorce. Stifling feelings and frustrations about money can take a toll on marriage. Money can't buy you love, but many love affairs have ended over money problems.

Now is the best time to start planning. Whether you are newlyweds or are fast approaching retirement, this book is for you. Whether you have just started a family or will soon become empty nesters, this book is for you. Each of the chapters in this book is designed to get you and your partner talking and thinking together about your financial life. You may not choose to have an adviser. But you do need a guide for working it out when it comes to making important financial decisions.

It's hard to find the time to plan what's best for your money when you're busy trying to make more of it. In today's tight economy, putting in extra hours at work has become a prerequisite not just for career advancement but for keeping your job. At the same time, more people in their 20s, 30s, and 40s are becoming disillusioned with the rat race and want to find out how to spend more time at home while simultaneously having more money to spend. It sounds like a magic trick. Where should you begin sawing the lady in the box? Your biggest expenses are probably fixed. It's difficult to pare down the costs on necessities like your mortgage, car payments, caregiving for your babies, and private schooling for your older kids. It's even harder to find the minutes, hours, and days required to start thinking about such things. Underpaid and overwhelmed, we find it hard to know where to carve out the time to turn for help.

The time crunch is the all-purpose rationalization that people usually use to explain why they haven't whipped themselves into financial shape. If you want to make the most of your body, you've got to start swimming, jogging, or going to the gym. You've got to start a routine and stick with it. If you want to get the most out of the money you make, you've got to get into a financial fitness program. You need to take up simple exercises that you can work through with your significant other to strengthen your family's finances.

Whether you're shaping up your body or your finances, you've got to set goals before you begin. When you join a new health club, before you can sign up for classes or use the equipment you may be asked to detail your fitness expectations. If you're a jogger or swimmer, you probably decide what distance you want to run or swim before you start each workout. Setting goals is also important in financial planning—whether you're trying to build wealth, protect your family's finances, buy a home, or preserve your nest egg. Establishing limits helps you pace yourself. Goals spur you to renew your determination when you miss them, and give you a sense of accomplishment when you meet or surpass them. Reaching your goal is the "big payoff." You'll be able to realize your financial dreams.

When it comes to reaching your financial goals, just as in most physical exercises, the first step is establishing your starting position. These stances can vary widely depending on your position in life. You could be a newly married couple or celebrating your 20th wedding anniversary or somewhere altogether different in your life. You will also need to factor in what you were able to accomplish financially—as well as what debts you've incurred—before you were married and how you've fared thus far. No matter where you end up, you've got to start somewhere.

Most likely you and your spouse fall into one of these four groups. Where you start often depends on where you've come from—your parents. The child of wealthy parents may find it more difficult to set a budget than someone who came from modest means. On the other hand, growing up learning about stocks and investments may make you more comfortable investing your own money.

Negative newlyweds. Many young couples face a financial squeeze even before they tie the knot. Alice, a part-time student and stay-at-home mom, was burdened by student loans and credit card debt long before her husband, Michael, walked her down the aisle. When they married, their financial load doubled—as it turned out, he had his own crushing debts. Alice contacted a credit rating agency, and when she found out that her credit rating was extremely low she became too afraid to look into her husband's debts. The couple knew they had some monetary work to do when they got married. Now that the honeymoon is over, they don't even know where to begin.

Six-figure strugglers. It seems like you're living the dream. You've been married for 10 years or more and you're both getting sweet paychecks from your jobs. So why does it seem as if you're struggling to get by? Couples married for a decade or more may have found ways to whittle down student loans and credit card debt, but fixed expenses—the mortgage, car loans, health insurance, private school tuition—may have you living paycheck to paycheck. Even seemingly solid middle- and upper-class families are struggling. Take Mark and Janet. Together Mark, a videotape editor, and Janet, a design director, earn a mid-six-figure income. They drive luxury cars, have a nanny for their two-year-old son, send their daughter to a private nursery school, and moved into a million-dollar home six months ago. Nonetheless, Mark and Janet are walking a tightrope, balancing expenses and putting away little as savings. Mark and Janet's lifestyle masks the reality: they are stretched to the limit, with meager retirement savings, a tiny college fund for their children, and paltry reserves for emergencies.

Strength savers. Baby boomers close to retirement should know the importance of saving, but they still may wonder if they'll be able to save enough. They want to figure out how to kick their savings plan into high gear. The key is not to go too fast. In the late 1990s, financial planning for many couples focused simply on bulking up. Amateur day traders—many of whom were moonlighting in addition to their real jobs—dashed in and out of Internet stocks, buying and selling from E-Trade accounts. They watched their portfolios pump up during the tech boom of the late 1990s, only to see those accounts shrink with the crash that started at the end of 2000. Donna dabbled in a few of those high-flying tech stocks a few years ago. More of a risk taker than her husband, Theo, she thought she was a genius, sitting at her computer buying shares of Amazon and Cisco, and watching their stock prices go up. But when market conditions changed, the 50-year-old marketing executive learned a powerful lesson: developing financial strength means you can't focus on only one-day, one-week, or even one-year wonders. You have to take the time to research stocks, bonds, mutual funds, and other investments that fit your own investment horizons.

Future funders. Some couples figure they don't need a financial fitness plan. They don't overspend, they live off their income, they're saving for retirement, funding their children's college savings, as well as maintaining emergency reserves. They even have health, home, and life insurance. Like most Americans, however, they have no will or estate plan for passing on all their wealth to their heirs. Miguel and his wife have no plan for what would happen to their six-year-old son if they were struck by tragedy. The couple spent hours with their financial planner as he counseled them on how to protect their finances and preserve the wealth that they had built. But it still took them years to set up a trust and designate a guardian. The couple said it all seemed too complex and too sad to contemplate. And did we mention what Miguel's job is? He's an emergency room physician.

Once you've determined your financial position, you and your spouse can begin your financial workout to get into the best financial shape possible. There are eight exercises in this book with background information you'll need to complete each of them. Every one of these exercises offers straightforward strategies that you and your spouse can pursue over time to help achieve your financial goals.

These exercises don't have to be done in any particular order, but if you complete them all they should help you to devise a sound financial plan. Even if you are working with a financial adviser, accountant, or attorney to help you with your money, strengthening your financial muscles on your own is essential to reaching your goals.

This isn't busywork and this isn't homework. This is lifework.

I use these exercises myself, and they have really helped. Does my husband still doze off when it comes to financial matters? He sure does. But I've also learned that, despite his monetary narcolepsy, we share the same dreams. He may not be as outwardly enthusiastic—or get as stressed out as I do—about financial concerns. But he is also focused on earning extra income to supplement our salaries and increasing the amount of money we are able to save for our retirement, our children's college years, as well as our annual vacation (preferably to a warm, sunny beach in Jamaica). These exercises were key in helping us to determine what our budget wants and needs really were. By using them, we were able to get a conversation going about our personal finances. And we have been able to start down the road toward reaching our financial goals and realizing our financial dreams.

After working hard to provide for your family, the reward of discovering your financial strength will also bring peace of mind—so you can enjoy your marriage, your family, and your lives. That's the Big Payoff!

Let's get started.

1

ENERGIZER BUNNY MONEY
Stretch Your Budget and Make Your Money Last and Last and Last.

It's a conversation that most couples put off as long as they can. Most of them never get up the nerve to have it. Each person may have an imaginary version of the discussion—at many different times, in many different versions—in their head over the course of the years and the relationship. But it's devilishly difficult to find the right time, if there ever is a right time, to have the talk.

It's the love handles talk.

Most women have asked their mates, at one time or another, "Do I look fat in this?" The correct answer, of course, is always "No—you look great!" no matter what the truth actually is. The fact of the matter is that almost everyone gains weight over the years. And many people notice their partner packing on the pounds as time goes by. One or both of you may have a health club membership. More than likely neither of you is religiously using it. Perhaps you were devout about working out at first. But now, with kids, work and more, when it comes to working out, you're an agnostic at best. And neither you nor your significant other ever talks about it. You just keep on keeping on, leaving the top button of your pants undone and hanging your blouse over your waistline, or buying new outfits when you can spare a moment, which is never.

Personal finance is like personal fitness. We let ourselves go because we seem never to have the time, and it's too difficult to bring up the subject anyway. Getting in financial shape is tough. It requires focus, planning, and lots of sweat. But the end result will be a happier, more fulfilling life. Starting today, you need to make a commitment to manage your money and not let it manage you—the earlier you start, the better, although it's never too late to begin.

You need to have a talk with your spouse about the love handles that your finances have been developing.

If you haven't exercised in a while, your muscles can be tight and later you may notice the muscles you haven't used in so long are a little sore. As you begin "stretching your budget," you may find this exercise is also a little painful at first as you come to terms with what you can and cannot afford. But in the long run, some discomfort in the beginning can lead to a significant financial gain down the road. Like any serious workout, constructing and maintaining a budget requires a high degree of discipline. A budget is perceived as a limiting factor rather than a plan that leads to financial success. Since many couples are not good at managing their money, they simply want to avoid the issue. Most people will say they don't have time to create and follow a budget. Some just aren't sure how to go about it.

This chapter will show you that creating a budget is actually pretty simple. You just need to figure out how much money is coming in every month (your income) and how much is going out (your expenses). That's a basic budget. But the key for couples is to keep that budget somewhat flexible, based on your wants and needs and your spouse's (and kids', too!). You need to *talk* about your budget—not just put it on paper. That may be the hardest part. Even couples that communicate well about other topics are not great at talking (calmly) about money. This chapter has some strategies that should help.

When it comes to working out your finances as a couple, you have to keep those financial muscles flexible. You may have your own dreams and goals, but the more rigid you are, the tougher it will be to work together to realize those financial objectives. The key to staying limber is to communicate. Talk it out with one another. Identify your dreams and goals. Share them with your partner. Discuss why they are important to you.

The desire to start a family is what got my husband and me to start working on our finances. I'm a planner by nature. I wanted to feel financially secure before I had a baby. I wanted us to have wills, set up separate retirement accounts outside of our jobs, and also create a "rainy day, one day we'll get a house, then eventually we'll send our kids to college" fund. We didn't have a lot of money, but we put a plan in place so that, we hoped some day, some way, we might. We didn't get these ideas from our parents. Neither of us grew up in households where personal finances were discussed very often. But both sets of parents—all educators—taught us the importance of caring for your family, because that's what they did for us growing up.

As in my own experience, issues that get couples to start discussing money matters and deciding that they need a plan of action are often life-changing events: the birth of a child, death of a parent, divorce of a friend, approach of retirement, beginning a new job or loss of employment. It can also be a relatively small thing. A husband buys a high-end remote-controlled car (price: about $350) and his wife is offended. She thinks his spending is getting out of hand and starts a discussion about their finances. Or a wife may buy a new Dolce & Gabbana dress and silver necklace and the husband decides *she's* spending too much money. So he suggests they need to start adhering to a budget. Another couple finally agrees they need a new SUV (they want a $42,000 Acura MDX, not another $28,000 Ford Explorer), so they decide to write down all of their expenses to figure out how long it will take before they will have the money to buy one. They decide to wait six months before making the purchase. In many cases, these "issues"—whether big or small—have become problems. To get the money-talk started, couples often need to realize there is a problem and then decide it's time to set some goals.

CREATING A BUDGET TOGETHER

When budgeting for two (or a family of three, four, or more), being organized is crucial. Getting started can be a challenge, especially if one spouse
is accustomed to handling financial matters and the other is not as knowl-
edgeable, or interested—a frequent occurrence with many couples. It isn't
always the partner who is making the most money who is the most interested
in managing it. A lot of folks enjoy raking in the cash, but don't have the patience for sorting it all out. Imposing a budget on the less interested spouse
isn't the answer. Both spouses need to work out a budget that encompasses
the spending and saving habits that will get them in better financial shape.
You may find that the two of you are able to stretch your budget very simply
once you've found out exactly how much money is coming in and how much
is going out.

So think of your budget as an ongoing exercise in communication. A
well-run budget can save a marriage before it needs rescuing. Some financial
advisers suggest setting up a monthly meeting to go over your expenses, using the time to go over the items you've purchased and to brainstorm solutions to problems as well as ways to increase your income. Which of your
wants are you willing to give up? If spending $10 a day on coffee means you
won't be able to go on vacation and a vacation is more important than going
to Starbucks, the decision to cut back on the venti skim lattes is an easy one
to make. (Instead, just try to picture a beach in Jamaica every time you gulp
down the tasteless-but-effective joe that's given out free in your office kitch-
enette.) Maybe you'll decide reducing your workweek one day a week exceeds the gear-shifting thrill of having a luxury sports car. (Plus, you'll be
able to cut back on child-care expenses.) The key is to make mutual decisions that are realistic. You may need to discuss cutting back on the clothes
you buy for work, change the way you shop for groceries (consider wholesale
clubs, buying in bulk, and comparing the "unit price" of items), or try out a

public school for your child for a year instead of the expensive prep school. But you both have to be open to communication.

Realistically, the two of you may rarely have a formal meeting about finances. For me and for Chris, our "formal" finance talks only happen when we meet with our financial adviser, but it seems we talk about our money issues and try to find solutions nearly every day, or at least every week. It's probably hard enough for most couples to arrange times for the family to have regular sit-down dinners. Conversations about your personal finances will probably take place in fits and starts: You read an article on Social Security and retirement in the morning newspaper or your spouse opens a credit card bill while going through mail in the evening, and it sparks a discussion. (And not, one hopes, an argument.) Setting time aside for a meaningful discussion about finances is often difficult, but it can be done. Try to find time in the evening after the children are in bed or before you get hooked on the latest episode of your favorite TV show to talk about your finances. (Yes, *Law and Order* can be put on hold for a night—trust me, there'll be another episode airing tomorrow.) Later, as emergencies and opportunities arise, you may have to alter your budget. But that creates another chance for both of you to reevaluate your goals and priorities.

A budget helps facilitate communication. It may not seem like that at first. It's not always fun to talk about who spent how much, on what, and why. Often, that's when the finger-pointing—and sometimes the crying, the arguing, the raising of voices, the slamming of doors, the eating of trays of cut-and-bake cookies to console oneself—begins. But getting all of your expenses out on the table lets you evaluate them all together, at once. It also creates an environment where you can both honestly express the importance of each item. How does each expense fit into your plans, priorities, hopes, dreams, and goals? Which of the items represents something that you *need* and which is something that you *want?* And frankly, anything that prevents you from eating trays of cut-and-bake cookies is probably a good thing.

HOW TO SET UP A BUDGET

The best way to set up a budget that will help you reach your future goals is to figure out what each of you is spending and saving now. You need to keep track of what money is coming in and what is going out. You may want to set up separate budgets and then compare the two. Be sure to do the following:

1. Track money that comes in. Collect your pay stubs and tally the money that you can count on every month.
2. List your expenses, starting with your savings. Remember to pay yourself first. Include savings for emergencies, retirement, and your kid's college education.
3. List your big bills next, such as rent or mortgage, car payment, child care.
4. Add up monthly bills that are about the same every month, including utility, phone, Internet, groceries, cable TV, and credit card payments (which you should try to pay in full every month.)
5. Brainstorm to make sure you include all other expenses. (Clothes, transportation, dining out, golf, hairdresser, pet supplies, etc.)*

Then review each other's budgets to come up with a comprehensive one that reflects your combined spending and savings.

(Quick tip: Get a large envelope to keep all receipts and pay stubs for the month. At the end of the month, write down everything that you spent money on and how much you spent. Compare that to your take-home pay. If the receipts total more than your pay, you've got some work to do. If not, make sure you note how much you were able to save that month.)

---

* *www.thebeehive.org*

What is the difference between *needs* and *wants*? *Needs* are things that you cannot live without, the goods and services that have the biggest impact on your quality of life: housing, utilities, food, clothing, child care, emergency savings, and home, auto and health insurance. *Wants* are items you desire but are not essential: cable TV, movies, eating out, a day at the spa, a new car, vacation. Understanding the difference between needs and wants is important when you are managing money. Most couples realize they need to have enough money for their mortgage or rent, food and clothing, but home or renter's insurance is also essential and so is having emergency savings, in case you lose your job. That means you can't spend all your money on things you want, like a spa vacation or a new car. Sometimes the selections are a bit subjective. Your spouse may think season tickets to the Yankees are a need. You may think they are merely a want. Or you may be of the opinion that the money is better spent on the Mets. These are the kinds of things you need to work out and should want to work out.

Determine what you desire (a summer house in Tuscany or an iPod with enough gigabytes to hold every CD in your local Wal-Mart or Best Buy) and what you need (a bigger home, life insurance, or a college fund for your kids), and have your spouse do the same. Then you both need to figure out what it will take to fulfill first those needs and then those desires. One way to do that is to compile a budget. A budget will let you know pretty quickly where you stand now and how far you'll need to go to reach your goals.

Sometimes the things that you want, you want out of necessity. They are really needs. How can you sort it all out? Here are five statements that will help you decide. Review them with one another. Which do you agree with? Which are really *needs* and which are *wants*? If you decide you *need* to be able to do all of these things, you may find your list of wants will have to shrink considerably.

1. I want to be financially independent by age 65.
2. I want to set aside money for retirement.

3. I want to make sure that we are financially prepared in case anyone in the family becomes sick or disabled.

4. I want to save money for our children's education.

5. I want to have a plan for what happens to our assets if we die.

Use the "Needs vs. Wants Worksheet" at the end of this book to make a list of items that you need and a list of items that you have each purchased just because they fulfilled a want. Then prioritize the list. Each of you should fill out your own worksheet and then compare how you responded. How much are you spending each month for these items? What is the total monthly cost of your needs? What is the total monthly cost of your wants? Are you spending as much or more for your wants as your needs? If so, try to identify ways that you can cut back on your wants in the future to save more money for the things you really need.

After you've outlined the cost of your needs and wants, look at what you are saving not just for emergencies but also for retirement and perhaps college for your kids. Are you living paycheck to paycheck? What is your immediate savings goal? Buying a house, a car, paying for your child's preschool? And what are some longer-term goals, five years or more down the road? How much are you saving each month to reach these objectives? Crafting a budget together offers an excellent opportunity to lay everything out on the table, and then set up a system of saving and spending that will help your financial life operate more smoothly. Once you set up a budget together, either one of you will be able to run it. If the person who pays the bills gets sick or has to travel for work, the other spouse can easily jump in. So if one of you enjoys—or at least, gravitates more willingly—to handling financial matters, the other spouse can still pitch in occasionally without being completely left in the dark about the couple's finances.

STICKING TO A BUDGET

Some couples don't think they need to keep a budget. If their checkbook balances each time they receive a paycheck—perhaps with some money left over—they assume they're not overspending. They believe that as long as they have enough dollars coming in to cover the household expenses and they've contributed to their employer's 401(k) *and* there is still a little money left over at the end of the month, then they must be on track.

But couples who sit down and make a detailed list of all of their expenses may realize that they didn't need to spend $600 last month on eating out, $250 on dry cleaning and $150 on CDs and DVDs. That's an extra $1,000 that they could have put into a retirement plan at work or an IRA, or contributed to their child's college fund. Maybe your immediate goal is to buy a new BMW or a condo in Florida or to vacation in Europe on your next anniversary. You both would have been a few steps closer if you had cut back on those expenses last month. Here are some steps to help you stick to your budget:

Get organized. Create a system that will work for both of you. Designate a filing cabinet or secured box for bills and financial statements. For some couples, paying the bills as they come in is much easier than letting them pile up and dealing with them all at once. A better solution is to do your banking and pay bills online. It's probably the easiest way to keep track of your income and expenditures and makes taking a 15-minute daily "financial checkup" virtually pain-free (except of course on those days when the big automatic debits—like your mortgage and car payment—are deducted from your account. Then again, watching your balance go back up on payday can make it all worth it!).

Instead of trying to remember bits and pieces of financial information— from the passwords for your online bank and brokerage accounts to the month you need to renew your auto insurance—write it down. Keep a section in a journal (or a special file in your computer) where you list the contact information for each of the financial institutions and professionals that you do business with (banks, brokerages, insurance companies, accountant, financial adviser, estate attorney, etc.). A calendar—that you both have access to—listing important dates and appointments related to financial matters is also a wise idea. You may also want to log this information in your regular daily planner, so that you don't miss important due dates.

Track your spending even more closely. Write down not only your take-home pay, but also the amount you are paying each month for each of these benefits and contributions—hopefully you are socking away the maximum amount or at least enough to qualify for the matching contribution from your employer, if you're lucky enough to work for a company that offers such a perk. Be sure to figure out what is being deducted for health and dental care and your 401(k), as well as for life insurance and disability insurance. If you are contributing to flexible spending plans at work to cover out-of-pocket health care costs and dependent-child care, write down those amounts as well. (This money will be used to defray the cost of over-the-counter medicines as well as prescriptions, doctor visits, and other health-related costs that aren't covered by your insurance. Dependent-child care contributions will reimburse a portion of the money you spent on day care.) For information and calculators on how to "stretch" your paycheck, log on to *www.mypaycheck.org* or *www.paycheckcity.com*.

Also, use your debit card for as many purchases as you can each month. It's one of the best ways to track your cash flow. Unlike a credit card, you won't get a bill at the end of the month and you won't have to pay interest on unpaid balances. But you will have a complete record of all of your purchases as part of your monthly statement.

Set goals for spending and saving. Review your list of needs and wants. Try this the next time you go into a store and decide you have to have that new flat-screen plasma TV or a salesperson tries to persuade you to buy that expensive pair of shoes. Walk away from the purchase and wait a week to see if you still want or need the item. If you decide to buy it, then check around to see if you can get it cheaper somewhere else. It'll be hard, but if you spend money *only* on what you *need,* and shop smartly for items you *want,* you will reduce your expenses.

After writing down your expenses, prioritize each expense based on your needs versus your wants. Determine estimated costs for each expense and set limits on how much you can spend on each item. If you have money left over after all the monthly expenses are paid, split the rest of the funds between savings and reducing your debt. Pay down high-interest credit card bills and loans first. Then put money toward savings, remembering to allocate for long-term goals as well as unplanned emergency expenses.

To complete your own detailed budget, go to the "Budget Worksheet" at the end of the book.

BUDGET COMMANDMENTS

Also, as long as you have a consistent method for keeping track of your spending and savings, you won't have to worry about one spouse imposing his or her financial decisions on the other. Lay down ground rules that you both will follow. Basic guidelines can help you come up with a detailed plan that is agreeable and attainable for both of you. These guidelines can also serve as points of reference to fall back on when you feel like you're starting to falter. Following these three simple rules—"the Budget Commandments"— should go a long way to helping you stretch your budget:

- I: Thou Shalt Live on One Income, Not Two
- II: Thou Shalt Pay Thine Own Self First
- III: Thou Shalt Stay Out of Debt

BUDGET COMMANDMENT 1: THOU SHALT LIVE ON ONE INCOME, NOT TWO

You can learn a lot from single mothers. Single mothers have to get by on one income. They have to take care of at least one, sometimes several, dependents. It can be tough living on one income in this economy. Yet more than one-quarter of the nation's 73.5 million children live with one parent and about 5.6 million moms stay at home, according to the 2005 Family and Living Arrangements from the U.S. Census Bureau. If you're a two-income family and you can manage to live on one income, the path to your financial dreams will be that much easier.

Whether you're newlyweds or have been married for years, the best way to budget is to plan to live on less than you both earn. If both of you are working, try to pocket one paycheck. Try using one income—probably the higher one—to pay the mortgage or rent and other household expenses, as well as car loans, and child care, food and all other bills. Direct the second income to savings. But don't skip contributions to retirement plans. If it's impossible to pay all of the bills and contribute to a retirement plan on one income, then dip into the second income—but make sure you are saving as much as possible of that money for retirement for both of you, as well as for emergencies (in case the sole breadwinner loses his or her job).

The decision to *quit* a job and live off of one income shouldn't be made without reflection, research, meditation, and possibly a short vacation. Women who are thinking about dropping out of the workforce should talk to others who've made that transition. Check out Mothers & More, a national network of 7, 500 stay-at-home moms before you resign from your position, just so you get an idea of what life holds in store for you if you choose that route. The workforce is like a plane at 20,000 feet—it's easier to drop out than it is to drop back in. And the trip down can be exhilarating, but you'd better know where you are landing and you'd better have a parachute. (You can learn more about the group at *www.mothersandmore.org*.)

WHEN TWO INCOMES BECOME ONE

There are very few absolute rules in financial planning. But here's one: whatever you do never quit your job without a plan. It's a rule that's worth repeating: *Never quit your job without a plan*. Resigning from a position with the vague orbiting notion that you'll find something better doesn't qualify as a strategy. Your boss may be a jerk, your duties may be tough, but hunting for a job is always tougher, and more boring. Sometimes leaving a job is a great career move. But if you leave one place, you should know where you're going next. And it's usually best if you have another job offer lined up, with a commitment letter in hand, or if your spouse has an iron-clad agreement for a promotion or raise.

Here are some key points to think about before you quit your job or as you try to figure out if you would eventually want to stay at home full-time:

1. Make sure you are able to live off of one income. You should have saved at least three to six months' worth of living expenses for the next job. And try to continue to save for your future goals.

2. Continue saving for your retirement. You may not bring in a paycheck as a stay-at-home parent, but you're still working and helping to support the family. You may no longer have a 401(k), but you can put any income that you do have into an individual retirement account (IRA), or your spouse can contribute the money for you. The 2007 cap is $4,000 ($5,000 if you're fifty or older), but you can augment those savings by having your working partner invest an additional percentage of his/her income for your retirement in a separate account. If you spend the bulk of your working years raising a family, for example, you want to make sure your financial future is secure.

3. Stay connected to the workforce by working part-time, working from home, or starting your own business. Many stay-at-home moms and dads remain in contact with their previous employers by consulting from home. More and more companies are creating initiatives to help parents balance work and careers. Find out what your firm has to offer.*

---

*"Cost of Being a Stay at Home Mom: $1 Million," by M. P. Dunleavy, *MSN.com*.

Living off of one income may seem impossible if you've been counting on that second paycheck. Most couples decide they can only afford the house they want or pay tuition for their children to attend private school or take family vacations each summer if both spouses are working. But living and depending on two incomes can be dangerous. Your budget is set—and often maxed out—on that combined income. What happens if one of you gets sick or loses his or her job? How long can you afford to pay your mortgage or rent and other bills on one income? What if you get pregnant? Even if your company offers some paid maternity leave, what if you decide you want to stay at home longer?

If you've based your budget for essential monthly expenses on one income—or even if you just live off one and a half of your combined earnings—you'll have enough money put away to cover those difficult periods. You may not be able to stash any cash in your savings account during those times, but you won't have to worry about how you'll pay your mortgage either.

By living on one income, you can also use the other income to fulfill other dreams and goals: staying at home with your children, going back to school, or starting your own business. The best part is, if you never need to dip into the second income, you may be able to tap into a sizable savings account that could help you whittle down your children's college bills and build a large nest egg for your retirement. As financial adviser Mo Barakat says, "The couple that can manage to live off one income and save the second is the couple that is headed toward financial wealth. That's the golden formula."

Many one-income couples may feel there is nowhere left to cut. Perhaps you can both look at how you spend your time and see if you can add a part-time job or do some freelance work to add to your earnings—and save that sum. Maybe you can't make a dramatic change in your spending and saving habits immediately, so start gradually. Instead of spending two incomes (or one income, if there is a sole breadwinner) down to the last dime each month, stash away 5% of your pay, then 10%, and work your way up to 20 to 25% of your gross income.

You may still think that is impractical or impossible in your situation. It may seem that way at first, but keep reminding yourself of the financial rewards. Save a portion of your income (whether it's 5%, 20%, or an entire salary) and invest it for the future. You'll be that much closer to your financial goals.

BUDGET COMMANDMENT II: THOU SHALT PAY THINE OWN SELF FIRST

The best way to start to save is to pay yourself first. You've undoubtedly heard this before, but do you and your spouse actually adhere to it? Do you have money automatically deducted from your paycheck each month for your 401(k) plan or other retirement savings programs? Are you contributing the maximum amount that your employer allows—or at least up to what the company matches if that is offered? Do you make monthly contributions to a traditional or Roth IRA? Do you have three to six months of living expenses socked away for emergencies?

Make sure your savings are diversified. Savings shouldn't be limited to retirement planning. Many couples contribute to the retirement plans and then stop putting any money away. They think that fulfills their savings obligation for the month. It's also important to save for a down payment on a home or a car or other items like unforeseen medical expenses.

If you haven't done so already, you need to start a savings account and deposit a set amount each pay period in an interest-bearing savings or money market account to cover these costs. Also be sure to take advantage of other employer-sponsored benefit savings, such as flexible spending accounts, which help cover uninsured medical costs and also lower the taxes you'll pay on payroll income.

The 60% Solution. Here's a great way to allocate your savings. Financial writer Richard Jenkins, editor in chief of MSN Money (*http://money. msn.com*), has boiled 20 years of complicated budget calculations into a

SAVINGS OPTIONS

EMERGENCY FUND—Money to cover 3 to 6 months of household expenses that you can access quickly (i.e., money market or bank savings account).

401(K), 403(B), 457 PLANS—Defined contribution plans that you set up with your employer; money is automatically deducted from your paycheck. Some employers will "match" your contributions with their own money or stock. You don't pay taxes on the money until you take it out. The maximum contribution in 2007 is $15,500.

TRADITIONAL IRA—an individual retirement plan that lets you each contribute $4,000 in 2007, plus an additional $1,000 each if you're age 50 or older by the end of the year. Contributions may be tax-deductible.

ROTH IRA—An individual retirement plan that bears many similarities to the traditional IRA. You can also contribute up to $4,000 in 2007 and $5,000 in 2008. Contributions are never deductible, but qualified distributions are tax-free. (Read more about these plans in Chapter 3.)

simple conclusion: He and his wife limit all essential spending to 60% of their total gross income. Most budgets have a great deal of detail. Web sites like MSN Money, CNN Money, *Bankrate.com,* and a host of others have budget calculators you can plug into to help you determine how much of your income you spend on housing, transportation, child care, food, and other necessities. Some calculators will analyze your spending on these items, for example comparing it with a national average based on your salary and the number of people in your household. But as Jenkins points out, in most budgets, there is too much attention to detail and not enough attention to the bottom line. Writing down every dime that you spend on a latte, your favorite CD, or a much-needed manicure won't necessarily prevent you from falling into financial ruin, especially since most of the biggest financial headaches are those really big expenses—like putting a new roof on your house.

After reviewing his own family's finances, Jenkins came up with a faster and easier way to structure their budget without having to account for every penny. He decided they needed to keep "committed expenses" at or below 60% of their gross income (their salary *before* taxes) to come out ahead at the end of the month. *Take a look at the Budget Worksheet at the end of the book first.* Depending on your "commitments," the number may be higher (probably much higher) or lower for you and your spouse. But 60% is probably a good place to start.

Committed expenses (covering 60% of gross income) would include:

- All taxes (including taxes withheld from pay)
- Essential household expenses: rent or mortgage, home insurance, real estate taxes, phone, utilities (gas, water, electric), other household expenses
- Basic food, clothing, transportation: groceries, dry cleaning, auto loan, auto insurance, gasoline
- Insurance premiums: health/dental, life, disability, other
- All bills (child care, education, other committed expenses)

Then, divide the remaining 40% of your gross income into four chunks—split evenly or weighed according to your objectives:

Retirement savings. Have automatic payroll deductions (or deductions from your checking account) of at least 10% of your income made into a 401(k), 403(b), Roth, or traditional IRA, or self-employed retirement plan (SEP-IRA, SIMPLE IRA, solo 401(k)).

Long-term savings/emergency fund. Invest 10% in stocks and bonds, but keep most of this money liquid so that cash could be available in case of emergency.

Short-term savings. Money should be direct-deposited from your paycheck to a money market or interest-bearing savings account. Use this money to pay discretionary expenses for vacations, repairs, new appliances, holiday gifts, charitable contributions, and other irregular, but predictable, expenses.

Fun money. Spend it on anything you like, but don't exceed 10% of gross income. You could also make a budget for just three categories: committed expenses, fun money, and irregular expenses—and save 20% of your income for long-term goals, such as retirement and/or college savings. If you can manage to save 10 to 20% of your income, you will be amazed at what you will be able to accomplish in the years ahead. *You can make your own 60% Solution Budget using the worksheet at the end of the book.*

Remember that this budget is based on your *gross* income, not after-tax income. Still, keeping Committed Expenses to 60% of your gross income may be impossible, at least initially. That's probably because you're over-committed. Many couples have too much mortgage, too much debt, big car payments, and private school tuition that they really can't afford. If you're in a position where you receive an annual raise or bonus above the rate of inflation, Jenkins suggests you just hold your Committed Expenses steady for a while and let the raises or bonuses reduce the percentage over time. Otherwise, you will have to look at ways to reduce those expenses.

For couples saddled with student loans and huge credit card bills the first impulse may be to let saving for the future take a backseat while you pay off your debt. But considering the amount of money you'll need for retirement—as much as 100% or more of your current income by the time you reach age 67—it's important to start saving as early as possible. If you don't feel comfortable contributing a full 20% of your income to retirement and long-term savings, at least stash the maximum into your employer's retirement savings account, an IRA or self-employed retirement plan. Any money left over from that 20% pot can go toward paying down your debt.

This is not a rich person's budget. Says Jenkins: "I've gotten mail from people who are making it work on as little as $31,000 per year. The key is keeping a lid on housing and transportation costs."

With the "60% Solution," you don't really need to track your expenses because your checking account balance should ideally be equal to the amount of money that you will spend each month. A lot of couples budget that way—spending down to the last dime in their checking account each month—the problem is they don't make provisions for savings first.

In following the 60% Solution, you may find that Jenkins is right in his assertion that the real secret to building a budget isn't tracking what you

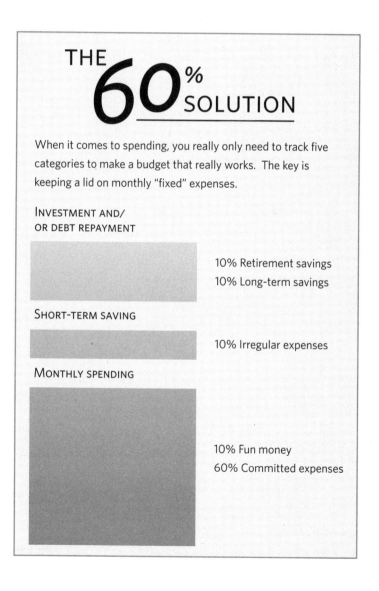

THE 60% SOLUTION

When it comes to spending, you really only need to track five categories to make a budget that really works. The key is keeping a lid on monthly "fixed" expenses.

INVESTMENT AND/
OR DEBT REPAYMENT

10% Retirement savings
10% Long-term savings

SHORT-TERM SAVING

10% Irregular expenses

MONTHLY SPENDING

10% Fun money
60% Committed expenses

spend (any more than counting calories is the secret to losing weight). He believes, as I do, that the key is "creating a sustainable structure for your finances, one that balances spending and income and that leaves enough room to handle the unexpected."

BUDGET COMMANDMENT III: THOU SHALT STAY OUT OF DEBT

Recognize your debt dilemma. The main reasons so few couples are able to save are simple: they overspend and they are in debt. It's not rocket science. Many couples today are taking on far more debt than their parents did a generation ago to provide the same standard of living—and adding even more debt to buy a house in an expensive neighborhood and to send their kids to private school and then to college. "About one in every seven families is in the same kind of shape that you are: having trouble paying bills at the end of the month, feeling extreme financial pressure, worried whether or not they're going to be able to keep the house and the car," says bankruptcy expert and Harvard Law professor Elizabeth Warren. For most couples, the only way to cover the mortgage, car loans, and other debt is for both spouses to work, and still they are stretched too thin.* Recognizing some of these early warning signs of financial trouble identified by the National Foundation for Credit Counseling (NFCC) could prevent you from suffocating under mounting debt.

- You're behind on the basics, like the mortgage or rent, and utility bills.
- You're using credit to buy items you should be able to buy with cash, like groceries. (You may say you're using the plastic to get frequent flier miles or rewards points that the card offers. But if you're not

---

*Maryanne Murray Buechner, "Parent Trap: Want to Go Bust? Have a Kid. Educate Same. Why the Middle Class Never Had It So Bad," *Time,* September 9, 2003.

paying that credit card bill in full each month, you're paying way more than that free airline ticket or stereo would be worth.)

- You're skipping payments on one debt to make payments on another bill.
- You're receiving overdue notices or telephone calls from bill collectors.
- More than 25% of your take-home pay is used to pay back credit card debt.

Don't just suffer; take action and get help. Follow the NFCC's advice: Call creditors and let them know that you're having problems. Explain your situation and what you're doing to pay off your debts. Depending on the creditors' policies and your situation, credit and payment history, you may be able to negotiate your next payment or a lower interest rate. Remember, your creditors would rather keep you as a customer than lose you to bankruptcy and foreclosure.

DECREASING DEBT

Luther Vandross once sang that "A House Is Not a Home." Every homeowner knows the truth of that statement. A house is not a home—it's all about what you put into a residence that makes it a home. It should be about the people who live there. But a house is often a burden. A house is the reason you're eating in on Friday night. A house is why you're making do with basic cable instead of the premium pay channels. A house is why your kid is wearing a winter coat from last year and you're driving an SUV from the last decade. A house is a monster, and in a certain light, when you're in a certain mood, the upstairs windows can look like angry eyes, the garage can appear to be a ravenous mouth, and every time the garage door opens it can seem as if it's devouring your money and your happiness.

Your mortgage is probably the biggest debt you'll ever owe and the 30 years (even 15) it will take you to pay it off may seem like an eternity. But your house should grow in value over that time period; plus you can deduct the mortgage interest from your income taxes. That is considered "good debt." Student loans are also a more preferable form of debt. These are generally low-interest loans and the interest is tax-deductible. So if you're set on reducing your debt, first make sure to pay your monthly mortgage payment on time and the minimum on your student loans, and then start setting the record straight on the most damaging debt—credit card debt. Pick up two months' worth of credit card bills and calculate the interest you paid. If you pay off your credit cards, you will save that much every month. Once the debts are paid off, you can immediately redirect that money into savings. Here are some steps to help you decrease your debt:

1. *Figure out how much you owe.* Collect all your credit card statements and make a list that includes the interest rates, total amount owed, and minimum monthly payments for each of them. Put the one with the highest interest rate at the top and start paying off the bills in order from the highest to the lowest. Knowing the interest rate on each card is crucial. Why? Credit card interest rates can range from 0% for introductory offers to as much as 30%. So let's say you have a balance of $1,000 and your interest rate is 22%; it would take you 146 months (12 years!) to pay off that balance if you only made the minimum payment of 3% of the balance each month. During that time you'd pay $1,234.17 in interest. The same balance at 12% interest would take you 96 months (8 years) to pay off, and you'd pay $407.54 in interest. That lower rate represents a savings of more than 66%—that's extra money you could use to pay off other debts or contribute to your savings.* If you want to know how much you could be saving if you didn't have that debt, calculate the interest you paid for your last month's bill. If you paid off what you owe on your credit cards, you could be saving that amount every month.

---

*Melanie Haiken, "Nine Easy Ways to Lower Your Credit Card Debt," *Babycenter.com.*

You can use an online calculator at *Bankrate.com* to figure out how long it will take you to pay off your credit card debt.

2. Purge the plastic. Cut up your credit cards or limit yourself to just one. Hang on to the credit card with the lowest interest rate, but only pull it out of your wallet to pay for essential items. Using only one card will help you keep better track of your spending. Better yet, if you must hold on to one piece of plastic, make it your debit card (also known as a "bank card or "check card"). If your debit card has a VISA or MasterCard logo, you can usually use it anywhere those credit cards are accepted. But with a debit card, the money comes directly from your checking account so you're less likely to spend what you don't have.

3. Get the lowest rate. You may be able to get a card with a lower rate from the same creditor by simply calling the company and telling them that you want to cancel your card because you've been offered a better rate from a competitor. If you are on relatively good terms with the company, your creditor may offer you a lower rate rather than risk losing you as a customer. Otherwise, you can find a card with a low annual percentage rate (APR) by checking out these Web sites: *Cardweb.com, Cardratings.com,* and *Bankrate. com.* The Federal Reserve Bank also surveys credit card offers twice a year and posts the findings on its Web site at *www.federalreserve.gov/pubs/shop.* Be careful of cards with low "introductory rates," though. They usually last only a few months, at which point the rate can jump to 15 percent or higher. Unless you are certain you can pay off the balance within the specified, low-interest period, you're usually better off with a higher-interest card at a set rate.

4. Keep tabs on payment deadlines and annual fees. Late fees run as high as $49. So if you have three credit cards and miss payments twice a year (even by one day), you've paid an extra $294 that year (plus you'll have default interest payments to contend with). If you're running up on the deadline, call the credit card company. Many will let you pay online for free or over the phone with a check. The company may charge $10 to $15 for the service, but that's a fraction of the cost of a late fee and you won't get dinged on your credit report. Watch those annual fees as well. Lower-rate cards often have higher annual fees. So do the math to make sure they're worth it. *Bankrate.com* also has a list of no-fee credit cards.

5. *Pay over the minimum.* Credit cards often have very low minimum payments, so if you just pay that amount, you will be paying for a very long time. See how much you can pay over the minimum. Put that extra money toward the card with the highest rate. You may want to pay the minimum on the lower-rate cards to be able to make additional payments on the higher-rate cards. If two cards have the same rate, apply more money to the one with the largest balance.

6. *Consolidate your debt.* Take advantage of lower-interest cards by trans-fering your largest, high-rate balances and paying them off within the "in-troductory," low-rate period. But if you don't think you'll be able to pay it off in this short time period, don't transfer—because the rates are likely to sky-rocket. If you plan to keep switching from low-rate card to low-rate card, remember that this activity will show up on your credit report and may make you look like a bad credit risk. Also, keep in mind you will have to pay a cash advance fee, as much as 3% of the amount transferred, each time you switch cards. If you think you can pay off the "balance transfer card" in a few months, make sure you close the other card accounts yourself and tell each credit card company to note that your account has been "closed at customer's request." Otherwise it will look like the creditor closed your ac-count, another black mark on your credit history.

You also may have considered using a debt consolidation company. But be wary. If you're considered a credit risk, the consolidator may promise you an easy-does-it loan, with low monthly payments, and end up charging you higher interest rates than you're paying now—as high as 21% or 22%. Many debt consolidators build in a fee as part of the monthly payment you make to them (about 10% of the payment). They pass along your payment to the creditor—or debit directly from your credit account—and the creditor rebates the consolidator a 10 to 15% slice. So it's probably a wiser—and cheaper—

SMART DEBT CONSOLIDATION MOVES

1. *Take out home equity loan or line of credit.* Fairly low interest rate, currently in the high single digits, interest is tax deductible (if used for home improvements.)

2. *Do "cash out" refinancing.* Refinance property for a greater amount than you owe and use the extra cash to pay off your debt.

3. *Get a personal loan.* You may be able to get an unsecured loan from a credit union or online bank for much less than the current rate on your credit card.

4. *Negotiate better terms.* Call your credit card company and ask for a break. If you promise to make payments on time and stop using the card, the company may reduce your rate.*

*"The Basics: Your 3 Worst Debt Consolidation Moves," by M. P. Dunleavey, money.msn.com

move to try to negotiate a better rate and set up a payment plan on your own. Try the MSN Money Debt Consolidation Calculator at *www.msn.com* or *Bankrate.com's* Debt Pay-Down Adviser at *www.bankrate.com*. You can also get help from the National Foundation for Credit Counseling (*www.nfcc.org*), a nonprofit organization that offers free and confidential debt management advice.

7. Short-term savings can save the day. It may be a radical thought. But a last resort may be to use your short-term savings to pay off your credit card or other high-interest debt. Don't dip into your retirement savings or the kids' college fund—with the power of compound interest that money could grow substantially over the next 10 to 15 years. But if you have cash stashed in a money market account or bank savings for a rainy day, you may want to use it to weather this financial storm of debt immediately.

KNOW YOUR SCORE

Alice knew that she and her husband, Michael, had bad credit, but she assumed it was getting better. When the Florida mother of two was thinking about opening a neighborhood café, she ordered a copy of her credit report as she investigated different ways to finance this entrepreneurial enterprise. She was astonished to discover just how low she had scored. "I'd been paying my bills on time for seven years, thinking my score was improving," she says. But in fact it was lower than she imagined—and certainly not good enough for her to qualify for a loan to start her own business.

Alice understood that getting a better score would be crucial to landing financing to open a coffee shop. Why is your credit score so important? Because the first thing banks and other lenders do when you apply for a small business loan, car loan, a new credit card, or that mortgage for your dream house is check out your credit report and ranking. Your credit score, often called a FICO score (after the Fair Isaac Corporation, which calculates the number), gives lenders a snapshot of your financial life and can determine whether you'll qualify for that loan and how much you'll pay for it. The scale ranges from 300 to 850. The average consumer's score is 720.

When Alice checked out her score with one of the national credit reporting agencies, she discovered she had landed an abysmal 519. She logged on to Fair Isaac's Web site, *www.myfico.com,* to find out what she could do about it. Her report said she had defaulted on a student loan twice (in reality, it happened only once), and listed credit cards she didn't have. By correcting those mistakes, and continuing to pay her bills promptly, she raised her score to 700 within a year.

Even if you think you have your debt obligations under control, what does it say on your credit report? Does it reflect the new payment arrangement you negotiated with a lender? Does the report accurately reflect that those accounts you recently closed were "closed at customer's request," not

IMPROVING YOUR CREDIT SCORE

According to *myFICO.com,* a subsidiary of the Fair Isaac Company that calculates your FICO score, the most important things to watch for are:

• Accounts that are reported by only one credit reporting agency. Check to make sure such accounts are really yours.

• Accounts reported as late or derogatory on only one agency's credit report. Were you really late on that account? If you don't think you were late, contact the creditor and credit reporting agency to have the item investigated.

• Collection accounts or other negative items that show up on just one or two credit reports. Again, make sure these items are accurate.

Of course, paying bills on time will give you a better score. Keeping a low balance on your credit card can also improve your credit rating. Also to get the best score:

• Pay off debt rather than moving it around. Start by paying down your revolving credit. In fact, owing the same amount but having fewer open accounts may lower your score.)

• Don't open a lot of new accounts too rapidly.

• Shop for loan rates within a certain period of time.

• Apply for and open new credit accounts only as needed.

• Note that closing an account doesn't make it go away. (A closed account will still show up on your credit report, and may be considered by the score.)

Following these tips and correcting mistakes on your report can dramatically increase your score. And that increase can translate into huge savings by lowering the rate you are offered on your mortgage, car loan, or credit card. Check out the table on *myFICO.com* to see how your FICO score can affect your monthly mortgage payment.

the creditors'? Making sure that your credit report is accurate can save you thousands of dollars.

Your credit report, and the score that goes along with it, gives lenders a snapshot of your financial life and could determine the rate you get on a mortgage, car loan, or credit card—or whether you qualify for one at all. Potential employers may also review your credit history. So it's important to get a copy of your credit report every year and make sure it is accurate. You can get a free credit report each year from each of the three major credit-reporting agencies (Equifax, Experian, and TransUnion) by logging on to *www.annualcreditreport.com* or calling 877-FACTACT. Although you can get your credit report for free, you'll need to purchase your credit score either through *annualcreditreport.com* or directly from one of the national consumer credit-reporting companies.

- Equifax: 800-685-1111, *www.equifax.com*
- Experian (formerly TRW): 888-397-3742, *www.experian.com*
- TransUnion: 800-888-4213, *www.transunion.com*

This is one financial move that you and your spouse must make separately. Credit reports are created and stored on an individual level, not on a household level. Every married person has his or her own unique credit file at the consumer reporting agencies. While married couples may have joint credit obligations, most also have individual credit obligations (credit you opened and used prior to your marriage, for example). So share your credit reports and scores and then work together on improving them.

STILL BUSTING YOUR BUDGET?

If you've calculated and recalculated your budget and you're still spending more than you make, you both need to step back and reassess what expenses are putting you over the brink.

Housing. You may have a more expensive home than you can afford. This is usually the single biggest expense on anyone's budget, so cutting costs here can really help a couple trim their budget. Remember, a more expensive house not only comes with a bigger mortgage, but also higher property taxes, larger insurance premiums, hefty utility bills, and more maintenance costs. If your housing costs are eating up more than 25% of your income, you'll want to start making some changes to your budget. You're probably not going to want to move to a smaller, less expensive house—and you may not be able to do so in a timely fashion. But think about it.

If you decide to stay put, add extra money (perhaps from your long-term savings) to pay down your mortgage. Homeowners whose equity remains below 20% are still paying PMI, private mortgage insurance, which protects the lender should you default on your loan. Once you cross that 20% threshold, you should ask your lender to drop the fee. The law requires the lender to do so once your equity crosses 22%, as long as you have a conventional loan that originated or was refinanced after July 29, 1999, and you have a good payment history. If you have an older loan, you could be paying PMI unnecessarily without realizing it, adding hundreds of dollars to your mortgage cost each year.

Taxes. One way you may be able to add more cash to your budget is to double-check the amount of taxes that are withheld from your paycheck. You may like to get a big refund check in the spring, but by taking the right number of exemptions on your W-4, you'll be able to keep more money in your own pocket. If you are having too much money withheld, you're just giving the federal government an interest-free loan. Use the withholding calculator on the IRS Web site at *www.irs.gov* or W-4 assistant at *www.mypaycheck.org* to figure out if you are withholding enough or too much. With the help of current pay stubs and a copy of last year's tax form, you can see if you are withholding the right amount. Then, you can adjust the amount withheld from your paycheck by giving your employer a new W-4 form.

Transportation. Your car payments are larger than you can afford. This item can eat up 50% of your budget. Many couples who live in a suburban area with limited access to public transportation say they cannot survive without two cars to get to work or so that one parent can shuttle kids back and forth to soccer games and music classes. Since even an economy car costs about $500 a month, including payments, insurance, fuel and maintenance, getting a second car may have helped you bust the bank in this category. Use the online calculator at *www.commutesolutions.org* to calculate your costs based on your specific vehicle miles traveled in order to identify what you really pay to drive each year. Once all costs are considered, you may decide to sell the second car and buy something less expensive. Take good care of your car and keep it two or three years longer than you planned. Or, keep only one car. One of you can try using public transportation to get to work for a while. Also, consider carpooling with a coworker and sharing the travel costs. And, if you live or work downtown in a major city, walk instead of taking a cab.

Shopping around for auto insurance can also help you save. Paying significantly higher premiums every year, just to have a lower deductible, may wind up costing you much more in the long run. Your goal is to protect yourself against a disaster, not small damages. Increasing the deductible on your auto insurance could save you up to 30% on annual premiums, according to *Insure.com*. Also, combining your home and auto insurance with the same carrier could add even greater savings.

Children. Of course, you can't trade in your child for one who is less expensive. But having children often forces couples to move to a more expensive house (since housing prices are often higher in neighborhoods with better schools), and to incur higher insurance, food, clothing, and medical costs as well. And child care costs continue to escalate. You can't necessarily cut those costs once you have children—if you find someone or some place that takes great care of your kids, it would be foolish to skimp. But newlyweds considering having kids one day would be wise to start saving now. You can use calculators like the one at *Babycenter.com* to estimate how much you're likely to spend on your child—or just figure on spending an extra $10,000 a year or so per child.

One area where you may be able to cut costs, though, is private education for your child. Your children may be in a private school that you can't really afford. Costs of education begin before kindergarten. Parents send their kids to preschool in hopes of boosting their educational success in later years. Though two out of three kids now attend preschool, those schools are rarely publicly funded and may cost several hundred dollars a month. If you opt to send your child to private elementary or secondary school for religious, personal or academic reasons, tuition can cost $10,000 a year or more.

Even though you want the best education for your children, you may not be able to foot the bill. Borrowing to pay for precollege expenses means you're probably spending too much.

Lifestyle. The final reason that your spending is outstripping your income could be that you are simply living beyond your means. You want to live "the good life" and to you that may mean a big house, two cars, a couple of vacations a year. Many couples who are well educated and earn higher incomes often have a greater propensity to spend and they spend themselves into financial strain and debt. Consider reducing some of your regular expenses.

For most couples, the chief category for careless spending is food. In the first years of our marriage, my husband and I treated every other night as "date night." We lived in a Manhattan apartment with a very small kitchen and would eat out several nights a week. "Eating in" often consisted of picking up some prepared food from a local restaurant or deli. We reduced our food expenditures dramatically once we stopped eating out all of the time—though we added many more costs when we bought our house and had two kids. Still, cutting back on eating out has been one key to keeping our budget in line. We also eat more economically at work by bringing lunch from home or buying soup or a salad instead of a larger meal.

When it comes to grocery shopping, a frequent recommendation is to use a price book, just a little memo pad that you use to note prices on items you buy regularly, one product per page. Those who use these books say it is a way to stock up on items when they're truly on sale, not just when the store says they are. Some advocates say you can save as much as 20% on grocery spending by using a price book or writing down and comparing the "unit prices" of various items. While my husband and I are writers, I know that we would never take the time to do that. I prefer to shop online, where I can keep a "master" grocery list and compare unit prices for items very easily.

Television and the telephone are essential diversions in our home. Getting your cable TV, phone, and Internet service from the same provider can reduce costs. You may also consider canceling long-distance service on your home phone and using prepaid long-distance phone cards or just your mobile phone. Americans spend an average of $41 a month on basic cable TV service, according to Kagan Research. For premium services (HBO and Showtime, for example), you could be looking at a bill of about $80 a month. Disconnecting your cable, or at least switching to bare-bones basic service, could also save you hundreds of dollars a year.

Miscellaneous items can also be reduced or cut out: Find a cheaper salon at which to get your hair cut. Visit your local public library. If expenses for books, movie rentals, CDs, and books on tape are eliminated from the family budget—you can borrow them free from the library—that can add up to a considerable savings.

The bottom line in a budget is the same as in a marriage. Everything is a compromise and you each have to give a little to make it work. No compromise, no change. In order to create a budget or "stretch" the one you have already set up, you need to want to save—not spend. Since childhood, we have been bombarded with commercials and advertisements enticing us to spend, spend, spend. It takes a conscious decision—and sometimes a lot of discipline, too—not to spend it all today. It's important to save. Some couples approaching retirement or those who are well into their 60s haven't figured this out yet and they're still working as hard as they did in their 30s. But if you budget correctly, when you're retired, you can think of those overworked seniors—as you volunteer with a local youth group, travel the world, or go out golfing every day!

2

PRESCRIPTION FOR FINANCIAL 911

Create an Emergency Savings (Enough to Cover Several Months of Living Expenses) Just in Case.

There's a children's book by Dr. Seuss that I often read to my four-year-old son called *I Had Trouble in Getting to Solla Sollew*. It's about a young man trying to get away from his problems, so he journeys to the city of Solla Sollew, because they have few troubles there. But it turns out the one problem they have is a doozy. In the end, the young protagonist buys a big bat and goes home, to deal with his troubles. There's wisdom in that children's book. When it comes to hardships, it's best to play hardball. Don't hope for good luck. Plan for problems. That way you'll never be surprised, except pleasantly.

Most people plan for certainties. They store money away for retirement and for their kids' education. But smart savers plan for *uncertainty*. They budget for disaster—because it's the unexpected things that can knock you off your savings strides. Nobody can predict when an earthquake might happen; no one can forecast the exact date of a flood, hurricane, strike, or catastrophic illness. But one thing anyone can do is foretell that, at some point, and on some day, something will happen. Emergencies can sap your savings account and knock you back from the future you had planned—unless you're ready for them when they hit.

Many couples who manage to save regularly for long-term goals can feel powerless when it comes to staying equipped for emergencies. But without some backup money, it's not only the couples who live paycheck to paycheck who could be in financial peril. What if your partner loses their job, their car breaks down, their house catches fire, or they have unexpected dental surgery or huge bills from a prolonged sickness?

A couple's backup plan may be to pull out the plastic when an emergency hits. But that works only until you've maxed out those credit cards or fallen behind on payments. A single late payment can hike up the interest rates and trigger penalties that will make paying off the balance even harder. Imagine buying daily necessities like groceries and gas on credit. You could still be making payments on boxes of Lucky Charms you bought two years ago at 10 to 18% interest. Trust me, you don't want to go through life carrying long-term breakfast cereal debt.

Credit cards are no substitute for an emergency fund. A more sensible solution is to start saving. Squeeze another $25, $50, or $100 a month from your paycheck. Add another $10 to $25 each month, or every two, three or six months, as you whittle down your other debts. Slowly build an emergency fund.

Most financial advisers advise having savings to cover at least three to six months of living expenses, in case you lose your job, take an unpaid leave, or need cash to pay for unexpected home repairs or medical bills. Saving such a sum may seem like an impossible goal. A few years ago, a study by SMR Research found that more than 40% of American households have less than $1,000 in liquid, nonretirement savings accounts. Yikes! There is some debate over how much should be in your cash stash and what it should be invested in, but one fact is for certain: you'll need money to help you through those unexpected rough patches. One thousand dollars might not get you through next week. Keep reading to find out how you can create an emergency stash of cash, so that if disaster strikes you won't be in financial despair.

How Much Do You Need?

Some couples may be able to get by with an emergency savings of three months' living expenses, but I wouldn't count on it. Those who may not need as much savings include: (1) couples who don't have children, (2) working spouses with short- and long-term disability insurance that will pay a portion of their salary if they are unable to work, (3) couples who know they won't have much trouble finding a new job or earning more money when necessary, and (4) people related to Bill Gates, Donald Trump, or Warren Buffett. This is obviously a very small group. The rest of us need a cushion.

However, if you think you'll have a tough time finding new work, if you have kids, or if you care for aging parents, you and your spouse both should shoot for saving the max (six months' or more worth of expenses). The more people you support, the more likely you are to have unexpected or unplanned expenses. If you think getting hit with one emergency is bad, try getting slammed with two. If you lose your job *and* your spouse gets sick and has to take time off as well, you'll be happy you had the extra emergency savings.

So you're probably thinking: How can we save that much money and still contribute to our 401(k)s, put money away for the kids' education, and pay the mortgage and other expenses? Don't panic. Remember, you don't have to save three to six months of your *salary*—or both salaries—you just need to set aside enough to cover basic monthly expenses for your household. So if you skipped Chapter 1 and didn't sit down and set a budget, now is the time to get to it. *See the "Budget Worksheet" and "60% Solution Worksheet" at the end of the book.* You'll need to determine the cost of necessities, such as your rent or mortgage; utilities; groceries; car note; home, health, and auto insurance premiums; as well as debts you need to repay. Multiply your total expenses by the number of months you want your emergency fund to cover.

If you've recently married, perhaps you've moved into an apartment or

---

HERE'S HOW MUCH WE WILL NEED TO KEEP IN OUR EMERGENCY FUND

Grocery bill for 1 month _____ x 3 months = $_____

Gas/oil, electric, and water for 1 month _____ x 3 months = $_____

Mortgage or rent for 1 month _____ x 3 months = $_____

Car payment or bus fare for 1 month _____ x 3 months = $_____

Other debt payments for 1 month _____ x 3 months = $_____

Total amount we will need to keep in our emergency fund = $_____

---

home where one of you was already paying the rent/mortgage, utilities, and other major expenses. If so, the other spouse could pocket his or her paycheck to immediately start building an emergency reserve. Other couples should refer to the table above to figure out how much they'll need to save.

You could put away enough cash for a year or two. But most people don't since emergency fund money is usually put into a low-yielding savings or money market account and you probably want the bulk of your savings in an investment that yields a much higher return. However, if you know you will be out of work for a certain period of time, you may want to resolve to boost your reserves. I knew that I wanted to take at least a six-month maternity leave after the birth of my first child. Since my employer offered only six weeks of paid disability, my husband and I made sure we had an emergency fund that would cover the rest of my time away from work. I had two weeks of vacation time as well as my six-week paid leave, so thanks to an ample emergency reserve, I was able to spend a total of eight months at home with my son.

I must admit it was strange to go to the ATM, drain money from a checking account, and not have it replaced every other week by my paycheck. Instead, I refueled my checking account each week with a check from our money market account, where we keep our emergency reserve. Thanks to our emergency fund, I never felt like I had to rush back to work to make sure we could pay our monthly bills.

10 WAYS TO SAVE FOR EMERGENCIES

Once you've determined the total sum that you need to save and you've figured out how much you need to squeeze out of your take-home pay every month to reach that goal, here's how to make sure you put that amount of money away and keep it there.

1. **Start small by skipping the "extras."** Once you see where your money is going, it's a lot easier to figure out where to cut. For my family, forfeiting a few Chinese take-out meals and passing on pizza night for one month could easily add $100 a month to our savings. You can probably find at least $100 every month you spend on extras, and could do without, at least until you build up your savings. Another tip for the two of you: Try putting $1 a day, plus pocket change, into a large envelope or a jar. At the end of the month, you each probably will have about $50 to deposit into your savings account. Together, that's $1,200 a year (not including interest)!

2. **Draw down those no-interest checking accounts.** If you can't figure out where to cut back your expenses, consider cutting back the money you keep in your checking account. Most Americans keep too much money in checking accounts that earn 0% interest. That money's just wasting time. But you can fix this problem. Calculate how much your monthly bills are. If your bills typically are around $2,000 and your checking account balance is $10,000, put a least half of that balance in a CD or money market fund. An even better solution may be to close your checking account altogether and open a money market account with check-writing privileges. (However, some money market accounts limit you to a maximum of three checks per month, and don't allow checks to be written for amounts under $250.)

3. **Treat the emergency fund like a bill.** Only this "bill" will actually help you pay unexpected bills when you have no other income to cover them. These are the sorts of bills we like—kind of like "good" cholesterol. If you decide you need $6,000 or $12,000 in the fund, see how much you can afford to save each month and think of that sum as a bill. Write a check to your money market account each month for that amount. Earmark the check "Emergency Reserve" in the memo section.

4. **Have a portion of your paycheck automatically deposited into a savings or money market account to cover that monthly emergency fund "bill."** Another option is to have your financial institution automatically deduct a set amount from your checking account each month and deposit it into your savings account. Your financial institution usually can set the date of the automatic transfer for the day (or a few days after) your pay is deposited. Lots of couples systematically save for retirement, but not for emergencies, because the money comes directly out of their paycheck and goes right into their 401(k), so they don't have to think about it. Put your emergency fund savings plan on autopilot too.

5. **Let your emergency fund "bill" replace another debt that you have finished paying off.** Even when you've paid off that student loan, car note, or another debt, continue to make a payment for that amount to your emergency savings account. (Otherwise, you know you'll probably just spend it.)

6. **Quit using credit cards.** Unless you pay off your credit card bills every month, don't use the plastic. Getting rid of outstanding balances is a lot easier if you're not constantly adding to them. So pay off your credit card bills and, again, once you've wiped out that balance, write yourself a check for that monthly payment and stick it in your emergency fund.

7. **Limit your access to the emergency fund.** Segregate this money from the rest of your "spending money" by keeping it in a separate account, suggests financial adviser Michael Kitces. You may even want to open a new account at a new bank to emphasize that this is *special* money for an *emergency only,* he advises, and avoid the temptation of dipping into the assets. Another reason retirement plans are so successful is that there are taxes and penalties for early withdrawals. If stashing your emergency cash in a separate savings or money market account is still too tempting, put all or part of it into a certificate of deposit (CD), which will guarantee you a fixed rate for a set period of time and penalize you for taking the money out early. Even if you lose your job or have to foot the bill on a major home repair, you probably won't need immediate access to the entire fund.

8. **Boost savings with bonus money.** If you get a raise at work, a tax refund check, or a year-end bonus, deposit the extra money into your emergency fund. If you were already able to cover your daily expenses without that windfall, you won't miss it and the influx of cash could catapult your reserve to the top of your savings goal.

9. **Get the whole family involved.** Explain to your children that they have to contribute to the emergency fund as well. Instead of giving them an allowance of $10 a week, make it $7. Let them know that there may be fewer pizza nights, they may not be able to buy as many new clothes and shoes this fall, and will have to choose either karate or clarinet lessons this school term, instead of both. But also promise a reward for the whole family once the emergency savings goal has been reached: a day at the amusement park or a dinner at their favorite restaurant and a night at the movies, too!

10. **Once you've reached your savings goal, review your emergency fund every year.** If your expenses have increased, you may need to save more. Make sure you keep your budget updated so that you have a running tally of your monthly expenses.

WHERE TO STASH THE CASH

Your emergency money needs to fulfill three basic requirements:

1. Your money should be in a safe investment.
2. You should be able to access your money quickly.
3. Your money should produce income.

Most short-term cash accounts pay very little right now. Yet that safety is worth a lot when it comes to your emergency stash. Getting motivated to put money in a savings account that will earn less interest than the cost of inflation takes an incredible amount of willpower. Although you don't want to put this money at risk by investing in stocks and bonds, your hard-earned dollars need to be earning something even though they're just sitting around. Your goal should be to find an investment return that at least keeps pace with—and hopefully beats—the inflation rate.

Rates do change over time, but savings accounts, money market accounts and funds, and certificates of deposit are still the safest havens for your cash. To find the best financial institution for your emergency funds, don't simply compare rates. Also check fees. For savings accounts, look for a bank or credit union that has no account maintenance fees (which can sometimes run as high as $100 a year or more). You can usually eliminate fees by maintaining a minimum balance. If you have a bank savings or money market account, make sure the bank computes your minimum balance on an average daily balance rather than a minimum daily balance, so that you're not charged a fee if your account falls below the minimum on one particular day.

Here are some other places that will give you a slightly higher return than a traditional bank savings account:

• *Internet banks:* The highest yielding banks are not the Citibanks and Wells Fargos of the world. They're generally Internet banks, credit card banks or new banks started by insurance or brokerage firms. Rates on savings accounts at online banks, like Emigrant Direct, ING Direct and HSBC Direct, are usually higher than at traditional brick-and-mortar institutions. They don't have the same type of overhead costs and often offer better savings rates. Says *Bankrate.com* senior financial analyst Greg McBride: "The list of attributes to the accounts offered by Internet banks is extensive—competitive yields, lower service fees and bounced-check fees than brick-and-mortar accounts, more modest thresholds needed to avoid fees and a predominant number of accounts that are free or lack monthly service charges." Some online savings accounts allow you to transfer money online directly into your checking account. Customers say the biggest drawback to virtual banks is ATM surcharges, but since you shouldn't be withdrawing money from your emergency fund anyway that shouldn't be a major concern. Find the best Internet banking deals at *www.bankrate.com.*

• *Money market bank accounts:* These accounts pay a little higher interest than a savings account and are very liquid, which means you can get cash out quickly. Some accounts require a hefty minimum balance for the highest yield. They often limit the amount of transactions or free checks you can write without paying a fee. Also, take note of this important distinction: Money market accounts are FDIC-insured, which means the federal government guarantees up to $100,000 for each depositor.

• *Certificates of Deposits (CDs):* Putting your money in a CD means you're lending the bank your money for a specific period of time in return for a fixed interest rate. CDs come in different maturities, such as three months, six months, one year, five years, and ten years. Cashing them in early results in a penalty, but you can try to avoid this by what is known as "laddering" CDs so that one comes due as you may need it. The spread, or difference in interest, you'll get investing in a one-month CD versus a money market deposit account may not be much. You actually may do better with a money market account. But if you have trouble saving, the penalties you can incur when you take the money out early may provide the incentive you need not to spend. If you're already adept at saving, maybe CDs aren't the best choice. If not, this may be a great way to "self-impose" an additional savings barrier to keep from spending the money and really hold onto it for savings. Although CD penalties can be a few months of interest, they're generally *only* interest. Your principal, the amount that would be used for the emergency, is still safe and secure—so you should still have the money you need to cover the emergency.

• *Nontraditional financial institutions:* You can often find better-than-average yields on savings and money market accounts at branches of nontraditional banking institutions like MetLife Bank (*www.metlifebank.com*), as well as the finance arms of some of the nation's largest corporations, such as

General Motors' GMAC Bank (*www.gmacbank.com*), and General Electric's GE Money (*www.gemoney.com*). Again, check out *www.bankrate.com* to compare yields on savings and money market accounts. But keep in mind corporate money market accounts offer a premium over bank money markets because, unlike banks, they are not insured by the federal government. They're paying you a little extra to take on extra risk. If the company defaulted on its debt and went bankrupt, you'd have to stand in line with other creditors to get your money. Says *Bankrate.com* senior financial analyst Greg McBride: "There is no FDIC insurance on those accounts. As an investor, you've become an unsecured creditor of the corporation. Now that extra return is fine if you're willing to monitor the credit rating." You can check companies' credit ratings at *www.standardandpoor.com*. (The ratings run AAA, AA, A, BBB, BBB-, BB, CCC, CC and C-. AAA is the best rating, meaning the company has an "extremely strong capacity to meet its financial obligations," BBB means the company has "adequate" capacity to do so, BBB- is the lowest rating before noninvestment grade, and BB, CCC and CC are regarded as having significant speculative characteristics.) If the firm has a rating of BB or below, and you can't stomach any risk, stick to a high-yielding money market account from a traditional or online bank.

• *Local banks offering teaser rates:* If you prefer to have a roof over your money, you may be able to earn teaser rates that are higher than market average from small local banks that want to attract deposits. Check local newspaper and online ads or just ask your bank.

• *Money market funds:* Money market funds, offered by brokerage houses and mutual fund companies, invest in short-term IOUs of companies and government entities, and the rates paid on those securities move in tandem with the Federal Reserve's key short-term rate. They usually pay more than federally insured bank money market accounts. Money market funds are not insured, but since they invest in highly liquid, safe securities, most financial planners consider them relatively risk-free. The seven-day average yield usually quoted by money market funds is equivalent to the annual percentage yield on money market deposit accounts. Banks can often pay more than money market funds because banks can lend money at substantially higher rates than they pay depositors. Money market funds can only invest in Treasury bills, commercial papers and other ultra-short-term investments.

Another advantage of money market funds over money market bank accounts and certificates of deposit is that money market funds are available in tax-free versions. If you're in a relatively high federal and/or state income tax bracket, you may be able to net more interest through investing in a tax-free money market fund. If you own a money market fund with average or above-average annual expenses, you can boost your yield slightly by shifting to a lower-cost fund. Fidelity, T. Rowe Price, and Vanguard are among the major no-load fund companies with a broad range of money market fund offerings and annual expenses that are usually lower than average. Check out *iMoneyNet.com* for more info on taxable and tax-exempt money market funds, including those with the highest yields.

 ## CLIMBING A CD LADDER

As you're growing your emergency fund, consider keeping it in a money market account or fund until you have about two months of living expenses. Move one month of expenses into a one-month CD. When the CD matures, roll the principal and interest into another one-month CD. Continue to make your regular emergency fund "bill" payments to the money market account. When you have enough saved, invest in a two-month, then a three-month, CD. If you need to set aside six months of expenses, continue the process until you can purchase a six-month CD. Keep "laddering" the CD, so that as one matures, you can use it to pay for another CD. The number of "rungs" on the ladder depends on how many months of expenses you'll need to have saved.

But if you need more than one month's worth of money right away, you may face stiff withdrawal penalties. If the second CD you purchase doesn't mature for 20 days, yet you need that cash today or next week, you may be forced to cash in that second CD early.

HOW SAVINGS GROW OVER 5 YEARS			
	INTEREST RATE		
MONTHLY AMOUNT OF SAVINGS	2%	4%	6%
$25	$ 1,576	$ 1,657	$ 1,744
$50	$ 3,152	$ 3,315	$ 3,489
$75	$ 4,729	$ 4,972	$ 5,233
$100	$ 6,304	$ 6,630	$ 6,977
$200	$12,609	$13,260	$13,954

• *Roth Individual Retirement Account (Roth IRA):* It's better to have cash reserves than borrow from your 401(k) or IRA. If you lose your job, you may have to repay any 401(k) loans immediately or pay taxes and early distribution penalties on the loan balance if it's distributed by the plan. Withdrawals from traditional IRAs generally must be rolled over within 60 days, in order to avoid taxes and early withdrawal penalties on the amount. So don't dip into that. But, as a last resort, you may want to consider reaching into your Roth IRA.

(Note: If you need money for medical expenses that exceed 7.5% of your gross income, health insurance premiums while you are unemployed, college costs, or a first-time home purchase, federal tax laws do allow penalty-free withdrawals from an IRA.)

The money in a traditional IRA or an employer-sponsored retirement plan is almost always taxed, and also penalized if withdrawn before the account owner turns 59½. But tax breaks for the Roth IRA are different. Contributions to a traditional IRA may be tax-deductible. Since a Roth IRA contribution is never tax-deductible, you are allowed to withdraw regular *contributions* from a Roth at any time, tax-free, without penalty. All other

Roth IRA distributions are tax- and penalty-free if the distribution is a qualified distribution.

Ideally you should be saving for your emergency fund *and* contributing to a Roth IRA. But the reality is that many couples can't afford to do both. You still need to have a stash of cash that's easily accessible—at least half of your entire fund—which you can keep in a money market account. You can also put *some* of the money you plan to save for emergencies in a Roth. (The annual contribution limit in 2007 is $4,000 per individual (or $8,000 per couple) and goes up to $5,000 in 2008. Those ages 50 and older can contribute an additional $1,000 each. So a couple, both age 50 or older, could put up to $10,000 in 2007 and $12,000 in 2008.

You'll have to be more conservative with your investments than you normally would with a retirement account—no stocks or stock mutual funds— and remember this is the emergency repository of last resort. If you don't need it, if a catastrophe never arises, you'll have more money for your retirement. If you have to reach into the Roth, remember you can't replace that money (unless you are able to roll over the amount within 60 days) since Roth rules limit annual contributions. Still, using those funds could prevent you from struggling to get over a financial hurdle.

Savings accounts, money market accounts, certificates of deposit, and money market funds are all safe havens of varying degrees for the cash you'll need on short notice. Placing your money in them can be as easy as squirreling away savings in your 401(k); you can put your emergency plan on autopilot. You just have to get the money into the right investments.

3

ON GOLDEN POND

*Build Wealth Through 401(k)s and IRAs for
Smooth Sailing in Your Retirement Years.*

Jim, a 42-year-old auto technician, found fixing cars a lot easier than fixing a neglected retirement plan. When he was in his mid-20s, he started building his savings by tucking away small sums. As a young mechanic, he contributed to a union pension plan and later used an initial $2,000 investment to open a traditional Individual Retirement Account (IRA). At first, Jim invested his savings conservatively in a money market account, but soon transferred his savings into a stock mutual fund, which offered much higher returns. With steady contributions, his retirement nest egg had grown to about $12,000 by 1986. Then Jim got sidetracked. He got married, had children, and stopped managing his retirement savings. "There was about an eight-year period where I really didn't contribute anything to a retirement fund," he says.

Retirement is about finally having the time to savor your marriage, your children, and the fruits of your job. Ironically, major life-changing events like marriage, having children, or switching jobs can delay many couples from reaching their retirement goals. But at least Jim had an early start. In the retirement race, the tortoise (slow and steady) almost always beats the hare (fast but late). "An individual that gets started—even if he or she can't afford to invest very much money—at the beginning of their work career at 20 or 25 years old, they're generally going to come out better than the person that delays savings until he or she is 40 or 45 and can save two to three times as much because they have the time value of money on their side," says financial adviser Lorenzo Wilson.

There is value in building savings over time. Jim wishes he hadn't taken that break in saving, but his retirement fund still didn't fare too badly. Thanks to a strong stock market, by 1996, Jim had amassed a $30,000 nest egg. He opened his own auto repair shop that year and rolled over his traditional IRA into a SEP-IRA for self-employed individuals. With a SEP-IRA, Jim is eligible to contribute up to 20% of his self-employment income annually, but he usually puts away about 10%. His retirement stash now totals over $80,000. Still, he knows it would be much larger if he had saved for retirement consistently over the past 20 years. "It's a hard thing to discipline yourself sometimes to put money away for that, especially when you are younger, and I wish I had put more away," he says.

Still, by contributing to tax-deferred accounts, his retirement plan contributions have not only helped him save for tomorrow—Jim has also been able to reduce his taxable income today. That's why contributing to tax-advantaged accounts like IRAs and 401(k)s are such important components to building wealth. "You have to consider the impact of what your real return is—not just what you're saving, but what you're actually able to keep," says Wilson. "And taxes play a big part in that."

Jim plans to stash some of his retirement funds in a taxable account as well. That's his next step. "I'd like to do a lot of fishing and traveling in retirement," Jim says, and he hopes to reach that goal in the next 15 years. He wants to have enough money saved by his mid-50s so that he can stop repairing cars and start relaxing with his family.

Building Blocks of Retirement Savings

People are living longer than ever. That's good news. But retirement is growing more and more expensive. That's bad news. You don't want to put yourself in a situation where an early death is your best financial option.

Now is the time—no matter what period of life you're in—to get on track.

Regardless of your age or financial situation, these three rules should always guide your retirement planning so that your Golden Years don't shape up to be more like a Bronze Age.

1. Never dip into your long-term savings.
2. Be disciplined about how you choose to spend money.
3. When in doubt, or in financial trouble, see rule 1.

Following these rules is important to building wealth, especially since your opportunities to create wealth will inevitably decline as you grow older. Retirement is something you should be thinking about at the start of your career. The whole point is, by the end of your career, you should be so set up that retirement is the least of your worries. To start building wealth *together,* as a couple, you first need to discuss your retirement goals with one another. Your goals may have changed since you first started contributing to your 401(k) at your first job or since you initially bought mutual fund shares in an IRA. Maybe you weren't married at the time. Hopefully you started saving for retirement before you had children. But if you're married with kids, you probably are feeling the financial squeeze of saving for your retirement and your kids' college (and often, private school) tuition.

So take the time to write down your retirement goals now. Yes, right now. Get out a pen, a pencil, a laptop—whatever you have on hand. And get some paper, too. Got it? Good. Now put on some relaxing music—Bob Marley, Mozart, whatever. Now, start writing. Be specific. How does retirement fit into your overall savings plan? Is it your primary savings goal? Exactly what does "retirement" mean to you? Do you want to retire early or late? Do you want to continue working part-time? Do you want to move to a warmer climate? Do you intend to travel one to three months out of the year in retirement? Will you need to pay for your own health care (and your spouse's) in retirement? Keep asking yourself, what do I really want this money to do for me? Okay, we can pause for a bit. You can take a moment to listen to the music.

My husband and I started talking about our retirement goals a few years after we married. We both started contributing to company-sponsored 401(k) plans in our mid-20s, but didn't really pay attention to how much we would need to save in order to have a comfortable retirement. Initially we thought we would want to retire by age 55, but then realized reaching that goal would require us to save so much money each year that we would be unable to save for a home or for college for children that we planned to have. So we readjusted our retirement goals. We decided that we could work until age 67 (the year in which our full Social Security benefits will start to kick in). Even in our late 60s, we could still write articles or give speeches for extra income, but our goal is to enjoy our retirement together by traveling and spending time with our children—and, we hope, grandchildren.

We know that ideally we should be saving at least 20% of our income. Right now, we're saving about 10% of our gross income in tax-deferred retirement accounts (401(k)s and IRAs) and another 2% or so in life insurance with a cash value component that allows us to invest a portion of our premiums that we could use in our retirement. For the past couple of years, we've tried to put away about 3% in a 529 college savings plan (more on those later) and 2% of our income in a taxable account that can be used for our retirement or our children's college education. We're not saving 20% yet, but we keep trying to inch closer to that goal.

To reach your retirement goals, you may find that you have to increase your savings. Even if you've amassed a sizeable nest egg, most couples forget to factor in medical costs, which could substantially increase the amount of retirement income you will need.

SHARON AND CHRIS'S RETIREMENT SAVINGS

PORTION OF GROSS INCOME SAVED

10%—401(k)s and IRAs

2%—Cash value life insurance policies

3%—529 college savings plan

2%—Taxable account

17%—TOTAL

There's a shorthand formula some financial advisers use for figuring out how big a nest egg you need to finance your retirement. It figures you can spend 4% of your retirement portfolio each year, starting at age 65, without running out of money. (However, keep in mind the age to receive full Social Security retirement benefits is now 67 years of age, for those born in 1960 or later.) So the shorthand math would work like this: Assume you need $75,000 a year and that Social Security and a company pension would provide $30,000 of it. According to that formula, if you divide your unmet need

HOW MUCH MONEY DO YOU NEED FOR RETIREMENT?

Proposed retirement income	—	$ 75,000
Social Security and pension	—	$ 30,000
Unmet need for savings	—	$ 45,000
Divide by 4% (.04)	—	1,125,000
TOTAL NEEDED	=	$1,125,000

($45,000) by 0.04, you'll need to start retirement with a portfolio worth just over $1.1 million.

But math only tells you part of the story. You also have to figure something else into the formula: the Grand Canyon Factor. Most financial advisers have traditionally estimated that retirees need 70 to 80% of preretirement income to maintain their standard of living. If you or your spouse is in poor health or becomes ill, if you want to travel frequently, or if you just want to live more comfortably than you do now, you'll need more than that amount. Says financial adviser Brian T. Jones: "Most clients when they first retire plan on taking all the trips they have put off for a lifetime due to raising their families and work. They travel in the United States and they travel abroad. They are not looking for a reduction in their lifestyle at that time." He suggests couples shoot for having 100% of their household income when they initially retire, then 80–90% a decade later. "We have found that clients typically decrease their spending after the 10th year of retirement, when they are cruised out, have seen the Grand Canyon and been to Ireland," Jones says. "They don't want to travel that much anymore and prefer to stay local."

Start with your employer's retirement savings program (401(k), 403(b), 457 plans). Try to contribute the maximum amount that your employer and federal law will allow. Or, if your company will match all or a portion of your contribution up to a certain amount, contribute to that threshold. It's free money for your savings. It's unbelievable to me that couples who are aware of the need to save for retirement do not participate in company-sponsored retirement plans. It's a no-brainer. Many employers will match employee contributions dollar for dollar. That translates into a huge return on your initial investment. Says financial adviser Cheryl Creuzot: "An employee sets aside $1, gets a tax deduction, and *regardless* of the underlying performance of the account has a guaranteed return of 25, 50 or 100% given the match! Plus the account grows without currently paying tax." Again, it's a no-brainer.

If you're taking a break from your career or have recently quit or lost your job and are unable to contribute to a company-sponsored retirement plan, you can still invest in your retirement. Stay-at-home moms or dads may decide to delve into consulting or freelance work or start a side business during their leave. As a growing number of Americans become self-employed and create small businesses, they also become eligible for a range of wealth-building strategies, such as contributing to a tax-deferred SEP, SIMPLE IRA, or Solo 401(k), which can boost their retirement savings considerably. A spouse who is unemployed can also contribute to a Roth or traditional IRA on the basis of the working spouse's income. Don't worry, I'll explain. (More about those later.) So it is important to look at a range of retirement savings options to see which plan—or combination of plans—will allow you to build the most wealth.

If you've been contributing to a 401(k) plan at work for a while, you're probably like many workers who have at least some confidence about their finances in retirement. Unfortunately that confidence may be preventing you from making necessary changes to your retirement plan. According to the 2006 Retirement Confidence Survey conducted by the Employee Benefits Research Institute:

- One quarter of workers are very confident about their financial security in retirement.
- But 22% of very confident workers are not currently saving for retirement and 39% have less than $50,000 in savings.
- Only 42% of workers say they have actually calculated how much money they will need to save by the time they retire.

Rising medical costs can also eat up a huge chunk of your retirement savings. Benefits consultants at Watson Wyatt Worldwide suggest that today's workers may need more than 100% of preretirement income to pay for health care as employers cut back on retiree health benefits. Nearly half of employers surveyed by benefits analysts Watson Wyatt in 2006 cap their premium contribution to current retiree's benefits. Watson Wyatt says more future retirees will not receive any medical benefit at all—8% of employers plan to eliminate coverage for employees currently younger than age 65, while 14% plan to scratch benefits for those 65 and older.

Now consider that women today can expect to live until they are 80 and men until they are 75, according to the Centers for Disease Control and Prevention. Many individuals will spend a decade or two, maybe even more, in retirement. To estimate your life span as accurately as possible, you need to consider your nutrition, family history, health and lifestyle, as well as environmental issues. The "Living to 100 Healthspan Calculator," at *www.livingto100.com,* is a great tool that takes these factors into account. So there is reason to be concerned because for those who are not prepared, there is a real risk of outliving your retirement savings.

The rate of health care cost increases will also affect your retirement expenses. Forecasts have shown that cost increases should moderate to about 10% a year over the long term. But you and your spouse may wind up shouldering more of those expenses in retirement than you do now. Even if your employer or your spouse's employer offers retiree benefits now, plans are changing rapidly, requiring you to save even more. If you turn 65 in 2016, given a 7% annual increase in health care costs, you would have to have saved $219,000 if you lived to 80, $409,000 if you lived to 90, and $656,000 if you lived to 100, according to the Employee Benefits Research Institute.

Don't plan on dying young? Living a long life is a good thing, or it should be. That is why it is so important to begin saving and building wealth as early as possible. The earlier you start, the more time you have to compound interest, even if you have a year with lackluster or negative returns, over time your money will grow.

The chart below shows how much you will need to save every month at either a 6% or 8% rate of return to build a $1 million nest egg by age 65, starting at various ages. These are just hypothetical rates, compounded monthly. These returns will not necessarily be replicated on actual investments now or in the future, but it gives you an idea of what to expect.

WHO WANTS TO BE A MILLIONAIRE?:

MONTHLY INVESTMENT NEEDED TO BUILD $1 MILLION NEST EGG BY AGE 65

AGE	MONTHLY INVESTMENT AT 6% INTEREST	MONTHLY INVESTMENT AT 8% INTEREST
25	$ 502	$ 286
30	$ 702	$ 436
35	$ 996	$ 671
40	$ 1,443	$ 1,052
45	$ 2,164	$ 1,698
50	$ 3,439	$ 2,890
55	$ 6,102	$ 5,466

SOURCE: www.investopedia.com/calculator/MillionaireCal.aspx.

You and your spouse need to define your retirement goals, including how long your retirement savings should last, and calculate how much money you'll need to afford to live in the style to which you have grown accustomed—or perhaps a little more spartan or luxurious, depending on how much you are able to save and the investments you choose. You need to develop an investment strategy based on *realistic* rates of return. If your expectations are too high, you may be forced to take greater investment risks or scale down your retirement lifestyle (more on that later). But you can start by fully funding all of the retirement plans to which you are eligible. Use the "Retirement Savings Workout" at the end of the book to tally exactly how much you have saved for your Golden Years. For a general estimate of how much money you will need to save to get the amount of annual income you hope to have in retirement, most financial Web sites have calculators that will crunch numbers for you. One of the most helpful tools is at *www.choosetosave.org.* Click on "Ballpark Estimate."

IT'S UP TO YOU!

Our parents' generation assumed that Dad's pension (and maybe Mom's too), plus Social Security would cover at least half of their expenses in retirement. For today's retirees that's pretty accurate. Those who are covered by company pensions receive on average 21% of their retirement income from those plans and another 42% from Social Security, according to a survey by Watson Wyatt Worldwide, the benefits consulting firm. Twenty-one percent of their retirement income comes from personal savings (including 401(k) accounts) and 16% from part-time work.

Unfortunately, couples today cannot count on their employers or the government providing nearly that amount of their income in their Golden Years. You undoubtedly have heard that Social Security benefits are dwindling. If you haven't gotten that news yet, feel free to take a moment and go to Google, Yahoo!, or any search engine of your choice and type in "Social Security" and "benefits" and "dwindling." Now that you've picked yourself off the floor, let's continue. In 2018, the amount of Social Security benefits owed to retirees will be more than the amount of taxes paid into the Social Security fund, and the system will need to begin tapping into its reserve funds to pay out benefits. Those funds are projected to be exhausted in 2042 and Social Security will not be able to meet all of its benefit obligations. So, unless changes are made in the system, by the time a 31-year-old of today hits the full retirement age of 67 (the age at which she is eligible for the full Social Security benefit), some experts predict, she'll get zilch. That's right, zero, nada, nothing, as in the check *isn't* in the mail. This may be an overstatement, as the Social Security system is expected by most experts to be able to pay at least a portion of promised benefits out of taxpayers dollars. But there's the real possibility that it could be the cold reality.

If you want to know how much of a benefit you're likely to receive, the Social Security Administration should be sending you a useful little document each year called "Your Social Security Statement." (You can also request one at the Social Security Web site, *www.ssa.gov*. It gives a record of your past earnings, plus three estimates of your future benefits: one if you retired at age 62, another for your full retirement age (see box), and a third showing what you'd receive if you waited until age 70 to start collecting benefits. The good news is you don't have to wait to your full retirement age to get benefits. You can begin collecting a reduced benefit as soon as you turn 62. But you'll get even more money if you delay receiving benefits until age 70.

Still, your Social Security benefits will likely make up only a fraction of the monthly income you'll want to live on. Considering the share of workers with defined benefit pension plans—the kind that your father had in which the employer contributes all the money and benefits are based on years of service and final average pay—is also on the decline (only about 20% of employees now have such a perk), you and your spouse will probably have to cover most of your monthly expenses with your own retirement savings. If the Social Security system gets fixed, consider those funds your "fun

AGE TO RECEIVE FULL SOCIAL SECURITY BENEFITS

YEAR OF BIRTH	FULL RETIREMENT AGE
1943–1954	66
1955	66 and 2 months
1956	66 and 4 months
1957	66 and 6 months
1958	66 and 8 months
1959	66 and 10 months
1960 and later	67

SOURCE: Social Security Administration.

money" for vacations, trips to visit grandkids, or courses at a local college that may inspire you to delve into a second career. Adequately funding your employer-sponsored retirement plan and other retirement saving vehicles already may be your primary savings goal—if it isn't, it should be. Remember, your kid can get loans for college, but there's no financial institution that will eagerly give you a loan to finance your retirement.

So where will your retirement savings come from?

You can build wealth and your retirement savings by contributing to several different pots. Once you believe you have a sufficient emergency fund (to

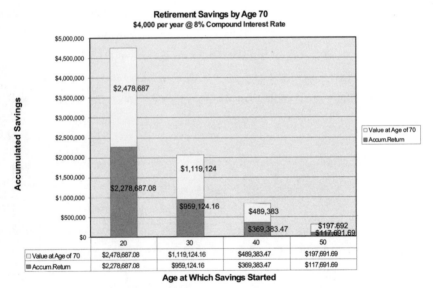

Retirement Savings by Age 70
$4,000 per year @ 8% Compound Interest Rate

Age at Which Savings Started	Value at Age of 70	Accum.Return
20	$2,478,687.08	$2,278,687.08
30	$1,119,124.16	$959,124.16
40	$489,383.47	$369,383.47
50	$197,691.69	$117,691.69

The data in this chart demonstrates the effect of saving at a steady rate of $4,000 per year, at an interest rate of 8% (compounded). The chart assumes no withdrawals are made from the account before the target age (70). It is important to note that actual interest rates and market performances on investments will very likely produce different results, which could be more or less than the accumulated returns included in this chart. Individuals should consult with a competent financial adviser for assistance with choosing suitable investments, and may also consider consulting with a retirement counselor for assistance with choosing the more suitable type of IRA (i.e. Traditional IRA and/or Roth IRA).

SOURCE: www.ApplebyConsultingInc.com

cover at least three to six months of expenses, in case you lose your job or are unable to work) and your debt is under control, then you should take maximum advantage of tax-deferred savings vehicles.

So start investing—or increase what you're currently saving, if it's not enough. Putting away the same amount on a monthly basis is the best way to invest over a long period of time. It really helps reduce the risk and volatility of the investments that you make. The example on page 58 shows the effect compounding has on retirement savings.

WHERE TO SAVE: DIFFERENT TYPES OF RETIREMENT SAVINGS PLANS

401(K)S AND OTHER EMPLOYER-SPONSORED RETIREMENT PLANS

Start with your company's 401(k) plan or another type of employer-sponsored plan (403(b) or 457 plan). Try to contribute the maximum. Automatic payroll deductions make this the simplest way to start saving and if your company offers a matching program (contributing money to your account based on the amount of money that you put in), that's "free money" to add to your nest egg.

If not the maximum, you should contribute at least enough to get your company match. If such a program is offered, it can considerably increase your savings. In 2007, you can save up to $15,500 in your 401(k), or up to $20,500, if you're 50 or older. Contributions to a 401(k) or a similar employer-sponsored plan, like a 403(b) or 457, are pretax, so they reduce your taxable income. A 401(k) deposit could save enough tax to pay for an IRA contribution, so you can save even more. (A new PERK: Some companies have long allowed employees to also contribute after-tax money to their 401(k) once they've reached tax-deferral limits. Now, employees may have more incentive to do just that when it's offered. Starting in 2006, earnings on after-tax contributions to a 401(k) also are tax-free providing certain requirements have been met!)

An IRA will allow you and your spouse to put away another $4,000 each in 2007, or $5,000 if you're 50 or older, for potential savings of $10,000. Among the great features of IRAs, they can be funded for the previous year until April 15 of the current calendar year. So if you forgot to make an IRA contribution last year and it's before this year's April tax deadline, you still have time. But don't wait down to the wire. The sooner you invest, the more time your money will have to grow. You have three types of IRAs to choose from: a traditional IRA, which can be deductible or nondeductible, and the tax-free champ, the Roth. Nonworking spouses can also contribute to each of these IRAs.

Deductible IRA. You can deduct IRA contributions from your taxable income if you and your spouse are not covered by a company retirement plan, such as a 401(k). If either of you are covered by a company plan, your eligibility to deduct your IRA contribution is determined by the amount of your income and your tax filing status. If your company offers a pension or retirement-savings plan in which you participate, the following applies: a couple with a modified adjusted gross income (MAGI) of $83,000 or less can still deduct their IRA contributions from their 2007 taxes. Married couples with a MAGI between $83,000 and $103,000 qualify for a partial deduction.

Nondeductible IRA. This is the only IRA option for workers who are ineligible to deduct traditional IRA contributions and earn too much to contribute to a Roth (see below). Contributions aren't deductible from your taxes, but taxes on the growth you've accumulated (earnings and dividends) are deferred until you make withdrawals. Still, you may get a better tax break by simply investing savings in a taxable account, instead of a nondeductible IRA. The top tax rate on stock dividends and long-term capital gains is 15%. Meanwhile withdrawals from a nondeductible IRA are taxed at your ordinary income rate, which could run as high as 35%.

Roth IRA. Even if you and your spouse qualify for a deductible IRA, a Roth could be a more attractive alternative. Contributions to a Roth aren't deductible, but if you wait until you're 59½ to take withdrawals (and it has been at least five years since you funded your first Roth IRA), earnings and gains are tax-free. Unlike other types of IRAs, you don't have to take mandatory withdrawals when you turn 70½. You can contribute to a Roth even if you're covered by a company retirement plan. But there are income limits. Married couples can't contribute to a Roth if their MAGI exceeds $166,000. If your combined income is between $156,000 and $166,000, you can each contribute a reduced amount.

If you and your spouse file jointly and your adjusted gross income is under $156,000, you should fully fund a Roth IRA. Is your paycheck directly deposited into your savings or checking account? Set up the IRA at the same bank. You can have the IRA contributions deducted from that account each month. Since income limits on a Roth IRA are higher than for a traditional, deductible IRA, it's a better option for many couples (see explanation of different plans below). Unlike 401(k) and traditional IRA contributions, payments into a Roth account must be made on an after-tax basis. But when you withdraw the money at retirement, you don't pay any tax if it has been at least five years since you contributed to your first Roth IRA. Contribution limits are the same as a traditional IRA. If you make too much money to qualify for a traditional deductible or Roth IRA, you may still want to stash some cash in a traditional nondeductible IRA. You won't have to pay taxes on the earnings until you take it out. Once you've set up the IRA, remember to fund it—at the maximum amount, if you can—every year.

If your combined income is more than $166,000, where Roth eligibility is phased out, put the money in taxable accounts. It may seem impossible to save any more and still pay your bills. But you should also consider setting aside a brokerage account for retirement savings and fund it as regularly as possible. You may not need it, but remember, you could also have hefty medical expenses in retirement (don't count on Medicare) and this account could be used to cover those bills.

Spousal IRA. Your spouse is working, but you're taking a break from your career to take care of the kids. You still need to save for your financial future. The same is true if you quit your job or were laid off or fired and are currently unemployed. Every married couple with at least $8,000 in earned income can contribute $4,000 each to their own IRA—deductible, nondeductible, or Roth. Those who are 50 and older can contribute another $1,000. Even if the working spouse puts money in a 401(k) plan at work, the nonworking spouse can still contribute to a deductible IRA, provided the couple's MAGI is $156,000 or less.

Take the money out of an IRA before you're 59½ and you'll have to pay a 10% tax on the amount, plus regular income taxes. But there are some exceptions. You will not have to pay the 10% early-withdrawal penalty if the distribution is used for any of these reasons:

- To pay qualifying health insurance premiums or medical expenses when you're unemployed.
- To pay for higher education expenses (tuition, fees, books and supplies, or room and board) for yourself, your spouse, child or grandchild.
- To pay up to $10,000 of the cost of purchasing a first home. In this case a "first-time home buyer" is someone who did not own (and whose spouse did not own) a principal residence in the two years before taking the money out.

Roth 401(k). A new savings option introduced in 2006 works like a regular 401(k) plan, but as with a Roth IRA, contributions are made in after-tax dollars. You won't get a tax deduction up front, but the account grows tax-free and withdrawals during retirement aren't taxed as long as you are at least 59½ and you've held the account for five years or more. That may be a huge benefit over traditional 401(k)s, especially for young couples who could see their taxes rise exponentially in retirement. There are no income restrictions on Roth 401(k)s. Contributions in 2007 were $15,500, plus add up to another $5,000 if you are 50 or older.

Converting a Traditional IRA to a Roth IRA. A traditional deductible or nondeductible IRA can be converted to a Roth, but a Roth cannot be converted to a traditional IRA. Any taxpayer with MAGI of $100,000 or less (except those who are married and filing separately) can convert a traditional IRA to a Roth. Income tax must be paid on the entire amount converted, except for any after-tax contributions. The amount that is subject to income tax upon conversion must remain in the Roth for at least five years—or until the account owner reaches age 59½, whichever is earlier—otherwise it may be subject to the 10% excise tax on early distributions. So if you're under 59½, and you convert your traditional IRA to a Roth, and then decide to use half of the money to pay down your credit card debt the following year, you'll have to pay a 10% tax penalty on the amount you take out, unless you are 59½ years old when the money is taken out, or if you qualify for an exception.

Rollover IRA. For many people, their retirement nest egg represents the largest share of their life savings. So knowing how it's invested and who is in charge of making those decisions is critical. IRAs typically offer more investment choices. With a broader range of options, you may be able to get greater diversification and potentially reduce volatility and risk in your account.

If you leave your employer, you may want to consider setting up a rollover IRA for this reason. And there are other factors to consider. Many employer-sponsored plans offer your beneficiaries limited payout options upon death. Beneficiaries may be required to receive a one-time payout of the entire amount in the account and pay income taxes on the entire sum. This could result in a sizable tax bill for heirs who inherit the plan assets. But IRAs offer your heirs the ability to spread the account balance and corresponding income taxes due over their lifetimes through annual payouts.

So keeping your retirement assets in an IRA instead of a 401(k) at your former employer could offer you considerably more flexibility—in your investments and in how the money is distributed when you die.

REASONS TO INVEST IN A
ROTH VERSUS A TRADITIONAL IRA

1. Roth IRAs are designed for retirement planning, but they can be a great short-term savings vehicle as well. There aren't many other tax-advantaged ways to invest your emergency fund or money for near-term goals. Unlike a deductible IRA, contributions can be withdrawn from the Roth at any time, tax- and penalty-free.

2. Setting up a Roth for each of your children is a great way to help them start saving for college or another long-term goal. As long as you can document that the child earned the money, you can deposit an equal amount of cash into a Roth with your own savings. But you can fund the child's account only up to the amount earned by the child.

3. If your tax rate in retirement is going to be higher than it is now, because of pensions, required minimum distributions from IRAs, and deferred compensation, paying taxes now on your income and contributing to a Roth might make more sense for you.

4. You can fund a Roth forever. With a traditional IRA, you can no longer make contributions when you're older than 70½. So if you're still working in your 60s and 70s (even if you wish you weren't), you can contribute and take advantage of tax-free withdrawals. Also there is no minimum distribution from a Roth after age 70½ as there is with a traditional IRA and if you don't need the cash, you can leave the funds to grow until you die. Then, distributions from the account are generally passed on tax-free to your beneficiaries.

5. If you're considering using your IRA to invest in real estate, but don't think $4,000 will let you buy much, you're right. But what about that rollover IRA from your previous employer? You can convert a regular well-funded IRA into a Roth, pay the income tax on the distribution, and then use the funds in the Roth to acquire a rental property. Rental income is deposited in the Roth and any housing expenses come out of the Roth, all tax-fee.

RETIREMENT SAVINGS FOR THE SELF-EMPLOYED
AND SMALL BUSINESS OWNERS

When you're self-employed, you have more choices about when you retire and how to save for retirement than if you work for a company. There's no mandatory retirement age, unless you set one. And you can choose from several retirement savings vehicles, not just a 401(k) and IRA. Among the options are Simplified Employee Pensions (SEPs), Saving Incentive Match Plan for Employees (SIMPLE) plans, and Solo 401(k)s, in addition to traditional or Roth IRAs. Qualified money-purchase and profit-sharing plans are also available, though they can be costly and complicated to set up. Even if you participate in your employer's 401(k), you can contribute money from a sideline business to a retirement plan for your business. If you run a small business or are self-employed, you should be able to contribute to one of these plans, and you could potentially save a great deal more than with a traditional Roth IRA.

SEP. With a SEP, you can make a tax-deductible contribution of up to 25% of the income you receive from your business (20% of your modified net profit for an unincorporated business), with a cap of $45,000. (Compensation is generally limited to $225,000.) You can fund the account until your tax filing deadline, including any extensions.

SIMPLE. You can contribute up to $10,500, subject to a cost-of-living increase in 2008. Those 50 and older can put an additional $2,500 in this plan. These plans have to be set up and contributions must be made by October 1 of a calendar year for contributions to be deducted from that year's taxes.

Money-purchase and profit-sharing plans. You can contribute 100% of your compensation or $45,000, whichever is less. However, only 25% of compensation is deductible and again, the compensation limit is usually $225,000.

RACKING IT UP TO GET INTO ROTH

Say your adjusted gross income is just over the cut-off to qualify for a Roth. Maximizing your deductions may just get you in.

1. If you're self-employed, work part-time for yourself in addition to your full-time job, or have any say in how your full-time employer pays you, try moving income from this year into next. Those who are self-employed may want to delay billing and collecting large outstanding balances into early next year.

2. Full-time workers should try to negotiate with their employers to move part of their salary and bonus into early next year.

3. Take advantage of flexible spending accounts, if your employer offers them. You put pretax money in those accounts so your contributions will reduce your taxable income dollar for dollar.

4. Or, if you're self employed and buy your own insurance, fully fund a health savings account, which would allow you to deduct over $5,000 from your taxes. And if you're self-employed, 100% of your health insurance premiums are tax-deductible.

5. You should fully fund your employer-sponsored retirement plan and self-employed workers have the benefit of putting away up to $45,000 for retirement in what is called a "Solo 401(k)" or a SEP-IRA (more on those plans a little later).

6. Finally, don't forget, if you switched jobs this year, unreimbursed expenses for a job-related move are deductible, as long as the new job is at least 50 miles farther from your previous home than your old home was from your workplace. If you can follow some of these tips, you may be able to lower your adjusted gross income enough to make you eligible for a Roth, and lower your tax bill too.

Solo 401(k). You can stash away as much as $45,000 in 2007, plus an additional $5,000 if you're 50 by the end of the year. The Solo 401(k) lets you defer up to $15,500 of pretax income, with an additional catch-up contribution of $5,000 if you're age 50 or older (just like an employer-sponsored 401(k)). Plus you can make a tax-deductible contribution of up to 25% of your total income (20% of your modified net profit for an unincorporated business), for a combined total of $45,000 (or $50,000 if you're 50 or older). With a Solo 401(k), you can roll over any other tax-deferred retirement savings into the account. If you want to use some of the money to reinvest in your business, you can also borrow against it by taking out a loan for half the balance or $50,000, whichever is less. You'll have up to five years to repay it. With a SEP, you may incur a 10% penalty and have to pay income tax if you take money out before 59½. Ask a financial adviser to help you compare your potential savings from a SEP, SIMPLE, or Solo 401(k). You can examine your options in more detail by checking out Publication 560 on the Internal Revenue Service's Web site at *www.irs.gov*.

How Much to Save

It may be tough, and initially impossible for some couples, to save at least 20% of their gross income for retirement—but that's the Golden Formula that many financial advisers suggest will ensure you save enough for your Golden Years. Depending on your situation, it may be more palatable to start by putting away 5%, build to 10%, then 15%, until you're able to part with 20% or more. Couples' ability to save will vary depending on their current household expenses and the lifestyle that they want to have in retirement, says financial adviser Michael Kresh. "However if they do not save at least 10% of their income plus fully participate in their employer's pension plans, they may not be able to retire at all."

If you're ready to start saving one-fifth of your pie right now, here is one way to do it:

Take a couple whose combined gross income is $150,000. Their goal was to save $30,000 last year. Daryl, 37, makes $100,000 a year as a manager at XYZ Corp. and Jane, a 32-year-old self-employed photographer, earned $50,000 with her business.

 SMART SAVING

Saving more for retirement doesn't necessarily mean you have to spend less—though hopefully you're already sticking to a plan (see Chapter 1). Here are some ways to save more without having to cut into your budget:

- *Refinance your home.* When mortgage rates are low, you may be able to cut your payment and send the savings to your retirement account.

- *Refinance your student loans.* Check to see if you can consolidate them at lower rates.

- *Fix your withholding.* Tax-refund checks will average over $2,000 this year. That's at least $166 more each month in your paycheck—money that could go into your 401(k) or an IRA. Change your W-4 at work so less tax is withheld from your check.

- *Reduce your premiums.* If you haven't shopped for life insurance in a while, you may not realize that premiums have dropped significantly over the last several years. If you find a new policy with lower premiums, you may be able to free up some cash for your retirement stash.

- *Pay the payroll tax to yourself.* Did you earn more than $94,200 in 2006? You stopped paying Social Security tax on any income above that amount. If you think you'll earn that much or more this year or in subsequent years, plan to earmark the extra money in your check for your retirement.*

---

*"You Can Still Retire in Style," *Kiplinger's Personal Finance,* March 2003.

XYZ Corp's 401(k) program matches 50% of employees' contributions up to the first 7% of pay they save. In other words, for every $1 that Daryl saves, up to $7,000, the company adds 50 cents. So the company's contributions can be as much as 3.5% of his pay. Daryl wanted to contribute more than that and decided to put away the maximum amount of pretax dollars that his company would allow a highly compensated employee to contribute: 10% or $10,000. The couple's adjustable gross income allowed them to qualify for a Roth IRA—so Daryl stashed away another $4,000 for 2006. Jane could have contributed to a Roth, but as a self-employed worker, she could save a lot more in a SEP or SIMPLE plan, or even a Solo 401(k). She opted for the SIMPLE plan. With a SIMPLE, she contributed the maximum of $10,500 for 2007. Daryl and Jane still needed to put away another $5,500 to meet their 20% goal. So they put those funds into a taxable account invested in a mix of stocks and bonds that they can tap into earlier than retirement age if needed.

ASSET ALLOCATION

Making regular contributions to your retirement plans still may not get you to your ultimate retirement income goal. You also have to carefully manage how these funds are invested. A few years ago, many financial gurus advised that over the long term you can expect your stock portfolio to grow 8 to 10% on average each year.

But many financial experts today say a more reasonable rate of return is probably 6 to 8%. Factoring in the bond portion of the portfolio, it's more likely to be closer to 6% annually—and that's not including mutual fund fees, which can bring that down to 4 to 5%. So review your asset allocation now. Morningstar's Web site, *www.morningstar.com*, is a good place for more guidance and tips on the mix within the stocks and bonds portions of your portfolio.

"ONE-SIZE-FITS-ALL" FUNDS

If you have trouble choosing from the numerous fund choices offered by your 401(k) or don't have the time to research them, *target-date retirement funds* are designed just for you. Fidelity, T. Rowe Price, and Vanguard have launched dozens of these funds and some 401(k) plans have already made them the default investment for participants who don't make their own fund choices. Here's how they work: Each fund invests in other funds and has a retirement target date. You choose the one with the year closest to the year you think you will retire. As that date approaches, the fund manager slowly alters the portfolio by adopting more conservative allocations. Yet each fund invests in a different percentage of equities at the retirement target date. Basically, the main drawback of these funds is that they don't take into account individuals with different goals or financial needs. Just because preretirees share the same retirement date doesn't mean they have the same retirement needs. Still, you may find the one-size-fits-all approach works for you.*

---

*"Retirement Investing 'Lite,'" *Consumer Reports'* Money Adviser, May 2004.

MANAGING YOUR 401(K)

For most of us, our 401(k) holds the bulk of our retirement assets, yet surveys have found that many plan participants have no idea how much money to save for retirement and allocate their money either by guessing or dividing it equally among all their available investment choices. That can be understandable in bear markets when stocks are tanking. Many 401(k) holders are so paralyzed by the fear of a downturn in their investments that they don't dare make any adjustments to their portfolios. They want someone else to handle their investment decisions, but they may not have a financial adviser. Some employers are stepping in to offer financial education and investment advice through telephone hotlines, online programs, and one-on-one counseling.

FINDING A FINANCIAL PLANNER

You may want some assistance with all of this. A financial planner can help. Here are some guidelines on finding one that's right for you:

• *Don't move too fast.* Chuck Jaffe, a personal finance columnist at marketwatch.com, says that when choosing a financial planner, don't settle on one too soon. Says Jaffe, author of *The Right Way to Hire Financial Help*: "For starters, don't just take any old recommendation. Do the one-on-one interview that you're supposed to do."

• *Do your research.* Barbara Levin, executive director of the Forum for Investor Advice, says: "One of the questions that is most neglected is: What kind of clients do you work with? Who makes up the majority of their clients? Because that will really tell you whether this adviser is used to working with people like you with the same needs."

• *Meet face-to-face.* Once you've found a certified financial planner, or CFP, you think you may want to hire, set up a meeting. Make sure you ask questions so you'll understand the services that will be provided. Go over any brochures or pamphlets that are available, and make sure payment arrangements are clearly defined upfront. Fee-only planners may charge you per hour or per financial plan or require you to pay a fixed fee based on your assets. Others may work by commission. No matter which you choose, Jaffe says, there's no such thing as conflict-free advice.

• *Stay involved.* It doesn't hurt to do a background check. Your state securities regulator can tell you if any disciplinary action has been taken against the adviser. Look on the North American Securities Administrators Association Web site to find the regulator in your state. Ask the planner or your state regulator for what's called Form ADV. It'll list any disciplinary actions and verify whether the adviser is a certified financial planner. And once you've hired the adviser, remember, you still have a responsibility to keep up with your investments.

Still, many workers don't have the time to study the investment options. Now, employers are stepping in to help by offering managed 401(k) programs.

"This is great for 'reluctant' investors, folks who don't want to spend a lot of time with investing," says Jeff Maggioncalda, CEO of Financial Engines, one of a handful of companies that manage 401(k) accounts. His firm handles accounts at corporations including Alcoa, J.C. Penney, and Motorola. To sign up, Financial Engines asks employees to check a box on the enrollment form it provides or call one of its investment advisers. The company will start to manage the account immediately, reallocating portfolios, if necessary, by choosing specific investments from the 401(k) offerings. The employee can opt out at any time.

So far, about 20% of all companies offer managed 401(k)s. If a managed account program is not available at your job yet, sit tight. Says David Wray, of the Profit Sharing/401(k) Council of America: "It is likely that within a few years, most companies will have some way for employees who don't want to make the investment allocation decision to have someone do it for them."[*]

Even if your company doesn't have the managed account option, if you're comfortable with online investment advice, you may be able to use an interactive retirement planning tool on your own on the company's Web site free, or at Financial Engines (*www.financialengines.com*), which charges a fee.

In order to take advantage of these services, you'll first need to get some information from your employer. The three steps to begin with are:

1. Review the investments that are available in your company's plan. Many employers often add new funds and withdraw tainted funds from their offerings. Check your plan's offerings at least once a year.
2. Figure out how much you can contribute. Make sure you are aware of the latest tax laws so that you can make the maximum contribution, if you are able.

---

[*]Sharon Epperson, "Does Your 401(k) Need a Manager?" *USA Weekend Magazine,* December 5, 2004.

3. You also want to find out if your employer will match your contribution. At a minimum, you want to contribute up to the company match.

If you don't have access to financial advice or don't have managed accounts at work, or if you are not comfortable putting this information online, you may be able to work with a financial adviser for a lot less money than you think. WiserAdvisor (*www.wiseradvisor.com*) a network of more than 1600 planners, is an online referral service that consumers can use to find a financial adviser. Of course, you have to conduct your own due diligence, including background checks and interviews. But the site can help you locate a handful of prospective experts.

It's worth keeping in mind that there are always reasons you can find to put off saving what you should. There are always unexpected expenses, setbacks at work, car repairs, home repairs, dental bills . . . the list is endless. But there are always better reasons to start saving *right now*. "There are going to be roadblocks that try to get in the way. Educating children, moving to a larger home; there are always going to be reasons not to get started," says financial adviser Lorenzo Wilson. That's the biggest mistake people can make, not starting early, and not focusing on saving. But you can't just assume it's going to be okay in the end. In fact, it won't be okay later. If you think saving is hard now, try doing it after you've aged 20 more years and have less energy, flexibility, and hair. Now is the time.

4

FEATHERING YOUR NEST

*Review Your Finances—and Ask
These Questions—Before You Buy
(or Sell) Your Home.*

Joanne and Matt looked at 30 houses on Long Island in New York, before finding the one they wanted to buy. Once they'd found their dream home, an elegant, yet traditional colonial, the first-time buyers panicked when it came time to finance the deal. The couple worried that they might be overpaying for the home at $592,000. But double-checking their bid against comparable sales in the neighborhood alleviated some of their concerns. "We saw houses right in our ballpark about a block away that were going for the same price," Joanne says. So offering the asking price didn't seem so far out of line. Joanne and Matt learned that doing a good amount of research not only makes sense—it may save you dollars as well.

Unless you and your significant other wind up purchasing a corporation or a country, buying a home will probably be the biggest investment you, as a couple, ever make. There's no polite way to put this so I'm going to just say it: you don't want to screw this up. Buying a home is a big deal. It's a major life moment, like marriage, or having a child, or giving up your Pittsburgh Steelers season tickets (bad move if you did this right before they won the Super

Bowl). It's also a difficult step, and a decision that's fraught with peril. You need to proceed with caution.

It is said that a person's home is their castle. But all too often, owners wind up being servants in that castle, when they should be rulers. This happens because they make mistakes going in. Getting into a castle is tricky—they're usually surrounded by moats. So people make bad calls, missteps, and they fall in. They pick the wrong neighborhood, so they wind up bypassing the nearby public school, which turns out to be failing, and enrolling their children in an expensive, hard-to-afford private school. Or they buy a home so palatial, all of their spare income—the vacation money, the car cash, the emergency fund—goes toward maintaining the mortgage. Or they buy a fixer-upper that's a real fixer-downer, a money pit that drains time, patience, and bank accounts.

Buying a home can be an incredibly emotional decision for some couples. You both need to take the time to decide what style of home you want, and most important, you'll need to calculate how much house you can truly afford.

Being flexible will also help. Your first home or even your second may not be your dream home and may not be a place that you intend to live for more than five years. "A couple might have champagne tastes and beer pockets," says Bob Moulton, CEO of American Mortgage in Manhasset, New York. "They have to see what their wish list translates to in dollars and cents. They may not have the money for the center hall colonial for $750,000. So they'll get a split-level for $500,000. They may have to settle for three bedrooms instead of four. They'll have to compromise."

And let's keep it real here: not everyone can afford the center hall colonial or the split-level for that matter. Home buying is like eating a good meal—it's a good thing if your eyes aren't bigger than your stomach. Get the place that you can financially handle. Then, five years down the road you may be able to "move up" into an even better home.

The emotions that come into play in finding a house can be overwhelming. You may find your Dream House—but the cost may give you nightmares. Your spouse may have no problem sleeping knowing that your ideal home will require taking on a $400,000 mortgage. Meanwhile you can't stop wondering how you'll ever pay off that much debt. Well, in many cases, you won't have to—you may not be in the house longer than 7 to 10 years. Still, don't forget that credit bureaus consider mortgage debt to be "good debt" and paying monthly installments on this type of loan can actually improve your credit rating and raise your score.

But there are other issues that you may not agree on. You may find that you and your spouse's tastes differ widely. You may need to compromise with each other and reevaluate your priorities in your search for the "perfect" home. After all, you are going to be living under the same roof. If you decide to buy an existing home, your desire for a house that is in "move-in condition"—which most buyers want—may not seem as important if you find a home that has a great floor plan and huge backyard for the kids. (Although picturing it with your own color scheme, hardwood floors and furniture, and without the pink shag carpets and dark brown wood paneling, may take some serious creativity.) Couples who build their own home may have to negotiate and compromise with each other even more, since decisions about countertops, tiling, and windows are compounded when you're starting from scratch.

Once you are in your home, the dilemmas seem to never end. After a few years, you may decide you want a bigger home. You may want to move to a different school district or relocate closer to your job or to public transportation. Can you afford to move? Does it make sense to sell your current home or should you put on an addition? If you decide to stay put, does it make sense to pay off the mortgage? There are a lot of questions to answer. So whether you are renters looking to buy or owners who want to move up to something better, you'll want to bone up on some of the basics of home buying and financing.

5 MOST IMPORTANT HOMEOWNERSHIP QUESTIONS

In this chapter we're going to discuss the Five Most Important Homeowner-ship Questions. Making inquiries is important. Finding your own answers will help you understand your home needs and your life. On the other hand, relying on luck might get you blown away. So here are the five questions you need to ask.

QUESTION NO. 1: SHOULD YOU RENT OR BUY?

Rent isn't just the name of a great musical and a pretty good movie—it's also a perfectly acceptable way of life. Don't attach a social stigma to rent-ing. Buying isn't always the best bet. Everyone's preference and financial situation is different and you may find that you are more comfortable rent-ing rather than owning. And, between you and me, it's not like anybody has to know. A rented home looks just like a purchased home. It's not like there will be a sign in the front lawn reading "Avis" or "Hertz." So don't sweat it, if that's the course you choose.

Compare renting versus buying—and, don't just rely on online calcula-tors. Online "rent versus buy" calculators don't always tell the whole story. They often omit or underestimate the total costs of owning a home. Mainte-nance, repairs, insurance, and utilities are almost always greater for a home-owner than a renter. And they may not factor in other savings for retirement or college. Still, the amount of money you spend on mortgage payments may be significantly less than monthly rent.

You're probably better off owning rather than renting if you:

1. Plan to stay put at least three years or more.
2. Are psychologically prepared to deal with homeownership, includ-

ing noisy and or nosy neighbors, clogged plumbing, a leaky roof, or whatever else may come up.

3. Have some extra savings (equal to at least two mortgage payments, and preferably much more).

4. Manage your money well (which is why it's important to get rid of your debt and make a budget before you start house hunting).

QUESTION No. 2: WHAT'S YOUR SCORE?

When you were a high school student, the most important number in your life was your SAT score. It determined whether you had a fun senior year or a desperate one, whether you got into the college of your choice or the safety school of your fears, and if your parents allowed you to drive the Mercedes or the Honda or forced you to ride your bike until you took the darn test again. Now you're an adult and you've got another most important number in your life. No, it's not your age. And, nope, the most important number in your life is not your cholesterol count. In my opinion, the most important number is this: your credit score.

Take a look at your credit report and score. You're entitled to a free credit report (a comprehensive look at your credit history) every year. But you have to pay a small fee to get your credit score—the number that gives lenders a snapshot of your financial life. Still, you need to see what lenders will see. "The credit profile of a borrower is a make-or-break factor," says Ted Grose, former president of the California Association of Mortgage Brokers. "It's the very first one that is addressed by any lender or mortgage broker." You can get a free copy of your credit reports each year from each of the three credit reporting agencies—Experian, Equifax, and TransUnion—by going to *www.annualcreditreport.com*. You have to go to the reporting agencies' Web sites directly or to *www.myfico.com* for your credit score, which costs a nominal fee. You want to see all the reports and scores because they can have different data. Most lenders say a score of 750 or better will help you qualify for the best loan. The higher your credit score, the lower your interest rate on your loan. You can also check out *www.myfico.com* to learn what rate you can expect based on your score—and how much you could save if you improved it. (See Chapter 1 for an example of how much you can save based on your score as well as tips on improving your score.)

Get your report and score at least six months to a year before you want to borrow so that you have time to pay down debt and challenge any errors in the report, both of which can improve your score. If you don't have much time, you can also ask your lender about rapid rescoring. Though it can be expensive, you may be able to fix mistakes in as little as 72 hours. The cost can range from a couple hundred to a couple thousand dollars, depending on the number and type of derogatory items in your report and how many agencies have picked up the information. "If a score is below 650, the money that you spend on repairing your credit could come back to you because you'll likely get a much lower rate from the bank," says Moulton.

QUESTION NO. 3: HOW MUCH HOUSE CAN YOU AFFORD?

Okay, let's get real again. In the postfeminist age, we're not supposed to acknowledge any difference between men and women. Let's stipulate that men and women are absolute political, moral, and intellectual equals. This we know. But let's also recognize that, when it comes to living quarters, men and women are different in many cases. Way different.

So it's important to find a happy medium between the sexes and find a place that you, as a couple, can both enjoy and also afford. It may seem like we're paying more than we used to for housing, but historically low interest rates (though they aren't as low as they were a few years ago) have actually made homes more affordable. If you live in New York or California, you're probably paying a greater percentage of your income on housing than couples in the Midwest. Yet, no matter where you live, some financial advisers suggest spending no more than 25% of your gross household income on principal, interest, taxes, and insurance.

Lenders used to stick to the 28/36 rule, which caps total housing expenses (mortgage, homeowners insurance, property taxes, and maintenance) at 28% of your gross income, and total debt payments at 36%. In today's competitive market, looser lending standards often allow a far higher debt-to-income ratio. That's a scary proposition. If, say, half of your gross income (or more) is going to pay your mortgage and other debts, you could find yourself eating macaroni and cheese for months.

So pay down excessive debts before you start talking to a lender. Make sure you and your spouse are already able to make your credit card, car loan, student loan, and other debt payments on time. If you get an adjustable rate mortgage or if interest rates rise before you are able to lock in a fixed rate loan, your mortgage interest rate may be higher than you expect—and those extra payments could seriously gouge your budget. So you need to make sure your financial situation is stable.

Complete the "Budget Worksheet" or "60% Solution Worksheet" at the end of the book to get a good handle on your current expenses before you go to a lender. Review your budget to help you and your spouse figure out how much money is available for a monthly mortgage payment. Write down your take-home pay, then subtract all expenses such as car payments, school loans, child care, retirement savings—everything. The amount that's left over will need to be enough to cover your mortgage and the ongoing costs of homeownership such as fixing the furnace or getting someone to mow the lawn. Don't forget to factor maintenance costs into your budget. (Like a well-manicured lawn? Lawn and garden maintenance costs averaged $387 in 2005 according to the National Gardening Association.) Go to the "Home Buying Worksheet" at the end of the book to help you figure out how much you both can spend for housing.

If you have enough savings to cover at least six months of living expenses in case you lose your job or face another financial emergency—or if you have a stay-at-home spouse who could go back to work in a pinch—you may be able to stretch and spend more of your income on housing. (Banks and mortgage lenders are becoming much more generous on the debt-to-income ratios.) Still, think about what you can comfortably afford. If you have large, fixed costs that you really can't control, like child care and health insurance, you may not be able to spend 28% your earnings on housing.

Use the "How Much House Can You Afford" tool on Fannie Mae's Web site, *www.fanniemae.com.* You can compare the monthly payments on different types of loans, as well as the tax implications, closing costs, and other fees. You can also calculate mortgage rates over the full term of the loan or just the number of years you plan to be in the home.

QUESTION NO. 4: WHAT IS THE TOTAL COST OF THE PURCHASE?

Buying a house, oddly enough, is a bit like staying at a hotel. The quoted rate may sound reasonable—it may even appear to be a big bargain. So you check in, a smile on your face. You send your clothes out to be pressed, order a little room service. You climb into bed and order a movie, maybe make a few phone calls. The next day, at checkout, after seeing the bill, you nearly have a coronary, an aneurysm, and a hissy fit, and not necessarily in that order. The base price is not the final price. This is true when it comes to houses as well. But you can always check out of a pricey hotel room. It's not so easy to check out of a burdensomely expensive home—unless you have rich relatives, diplomatic immunity, or membership in a witness protection program.

Consider all the expenses. Don't just focus on how you'll pay for the sticker price. Factor in how much you will pay in fees to actually buy the home—including attorney's fees, taxes, title insurance, prepaid homeowners insurance, and points. Remember property taxes and homeowners insurance can vary dramatically from state to state, town to town, neighborhood to neighborhood. And don't get caught without enough cash on hand at the closing. Closing costs usually average about 3 to 4% of the loan amount. Then consider that you and your spouse may need to buy a new washer and dryer or refrigerator or have to finance expensive home improvement, like a new roof or windows. Utility bills, repairs, maintenance, and insurance can also add up quickly. So as a rule of thumb, have a few thousand dollars in cash set aside to cover maintenance emergencies. Put it in the budget before you buy.

QUESTION No. 5: WHAT TYPE OF LOAN SHOULD YOU CHOOSE?

Interest rates can vary widely depending on the type of loan you choose. Rates on adjustable mortgages (ARMs) can be considerably lower than traditional 30-year and 15-year fixed rate loans. Rates on interest-only loans, where you are only paying interest on the loan for the first few years, can be even lower than traditional adjustable rate mortgages. But a fixed-rate loan is probably the safest bet. "It's great to be able to get into a home, but you need to be aware of the consequences," Moulton says. "Some couples are stretching and getting into homes that they otherwise couldn't afford. They may be destined for financial doom."

Here is a brief explanation of the type of loans that may be available:

Thirty-year and 15-year fixed. Payments are locked in for the life of the loan. Choose one of these loans if you're willing to pay for complete predictability. Interest rates are slightly lower on 15-year fixed than 30-year fixed. But, in either case, your payments won't change for the life of the loan. These loans are good for buyers who are likely to stay in the same house for at least 7 years.

Adjustable rate or hybrid ARMs. The interest rate is fixed for a set period (say 5, 7, or 10 years) and then fluctuates on a monthly or yearly basis. Go with this type of mortgage if you're willing to accept interest-rate risk in exchange for a lower rate and lower monthly payments. The shorter the fixed term, the lower the interest rate will be. It's good for buyers who are likely to move or refinance within a few years—or are comfortable with interest-rate risk.

ARMs aren't right for everyone. "People who don't think their incomes are going to increase or who really do believe they're going to stay in a home for longer than 10 to 15 years may be good candidates for a 30-year fixed rate mortgage," says Professor Chris Mayer of the Milstein Center for Real Estate at Columbia University. "People who use adjustable rate mortgages to get into a house, to get around the income ratios are really playing a dangerous game because if mortgage payments are that great a percentage of their income and they are adjustable, any kind of increase in mortgage rates could leave them seriously underwater."

Interest-only. You make only interest payments for a set period, then you add in the principal payments too. Choose this loan if you want to keep your payments down in the short term (at the expense of much higher payments later). Interest-only payments can reduce your monthly housing payments considerably. This type of loan is good for buyers who have received a bonus or expect to earn a lot more in a few years but are unable to afford the house they want with a fixed rate or regular adjustable rate mortgage now. But unless you plan to refinance, couples who opt for this type of loan should be pretty sure that their income will rise in the future so they can still make the payments when the interest-only period expires (usually in five to seven years) and they must begin to pay principal and interest—and those payments could skyrocket!

Piggyback. You get two mortgages (one mortgage and a home equity loan or line of credit) at the same time. For couples who don't want to put up too much cash for a down payment and also want to avoid private mortgage insurance (PMI), this is an option. If you have less than 20% of the purchase price, you'll probably have to pay PMI, which protects the lender in case you default on the loan. Once you've paid down your mortgage to 80% of the purchase price, lenders will cancel the PMI.

FIRST-TIME BUYERS

If you decide that you're ready to buy, the first step is to find a location that is suitable for the long term, or at least for several years. Since your home is an investment that could increase significantly over time, you need to plan to stick around long enough to see that happen. Think about how long you plan to stay at your current job and consider the employment opportunities in the area in which you will live. You'll need to be able to pay that mortgage. Even if you don't have children yet, ask neighbors, coworkers, and ask realtors about the area's school district and also find out about the town's development plans. You want to see if it is a place where you would want to stay.

Your house isn't only a nice place to live. It is probably your single most valuable asset. Yet many first-time buyers are so anxious to get into a new place, they overspend and don't do enough research to prevent other pitfalls. Here are some tips for making the big move a little less daunting:

GET PREAPPROVED FOR A MORTGAGE BEFORE YOU START SHOPPING

Find a mortgage broker or a loan officer at a bank or credit union who understands your needs as a first-time home buyer. You should like them, trust them, and know that they are competent—or the relationship won't work. To find one, get recommendations from friends and family, as well as your real estate agent. Make sure to get a complete assessment of how much home you can afford as well as the closing costs.

But before you begin to zero in on buying a home, you should get preapproved for your mortgage loan. This means the mortgage broker or loan officer must verify the information on your loan application and review your credit report. Once you've been preapproved, you can start working in earnest with a real estate agent. Since preapproval requires verification of your finances beyond just prequalification, it can also give you a little more leverage with the seller. But there is often a fee for preapproval that can vary with the lender. One caveat: A preapproval is usually only good for 120 days, and you'll have to update your documentation after 30 days, so get one only when you're serious about buying. In the last stages of the process you'll get a commitment or final approval letter.

START RESEARCHING NEIGHBORHOODS AND PRICES

Although you may need to adjust your search once you find out what you can afford, you can start gathering information on your favorite neighborhoods and home prices while you're waiting for the loan to be preapproved. Comparison shopping is relatively easy with a wealth of information available from several different sources: the Internet, newspaper listings, realtors, and open houses. Logging onto the Web and "Googling" various cities and towns is probably the fastest way to get information on neighborhoods, and school test scores as well as comparable sales. Watch for trends in the real estate market that you're interested in. If homes are sitting on the market for a while, you—the buyer—could have some leverage. If houses are moving quickly you'll have to act fast.

When Joanne was looking for her first home, her mortgage broker directed her to the Web site *Domania.com,* which offers a "home price check" where you can find out what the seller paid for the home as well as the sale price of other homes on that street or neighborhood. She was worried that she and her husband may have been overpaying for a home they found to buy. She knew that as a general rule, you want to avoid buying the most expensive house on the block, since it may limit your upside value when you decide to sell. But when she started searching the Domania Web site, she discovered houses about a block away that had recently sold for nearly the same price.

Domania.com, HomeGain.com, HomeRadar.com, and *Zillow.com* offer similar information, which generally will include the home's address, price, sale date, square footage, year the house was built, and number of bedrooms and bathrooms. Of course real estate agents estimate home values by finding comparable sales too.

FIND A REAL ESTATE AGENT WHO HAS EXPERIENCE IN THE NEIGHBORHOODS THAT INTEREST YOU

You want someone who not only knows the area, but also whose personal style, judgment, and experience are a good fit with your needs. If you don't feel good about the person, you shouldn't be doing business with them. It doesn't matter if they are with the biggest real estate firm in the area or just received their license. If you can't connect with that person and you don't think they'll show you the type of homes that you want, find another real estate agent. You may end up using several agents in your search. Most homes that are listed with a licensed real estate agent and are on MLS (multiple listing service) are available online at *www.realtor.com.*

There is also no law that prevents you from buying property without the help of a real estate agent. But remember, you are not the one paying the agent's commission—that is the seller's responsibility. You have the right to be an unrepresented buyer, but if you check newspaper ads or go to open houses, remember the listing agent usually represents the seller. So you may be at a disadvantage. The bottom line is an agent should be able to offer you a wider array of properties from which to choose, be an experienced negotiator, and be able to suggest home inspectors and closing agents and help you follow up throughout the closing process. You can do it on your own, but using an agent is your best bet.

GET THE HOME INSPECTED BY A PROFESSIONAL

If you think you've found "the one," but the basement smells damp or you see a few water stains, you still may not know if there is significant damage. Get an expert's opinion. You should always have the home fully inspected. Hire a professional, independent home inspector. If you anticipate major renovations, follow up with a contractor's consultation to find out how much money those improvements will cost you.

Many sellers have their properties inspected before putting them on the market. But if the home you want to buy has not been inspected already, include an "inspection contingency" of at least three business days when you make an offer. That will give you enough time to hire a property inspector and review his or her report. If the report turns up something unacceptable, you can cancel the purchase contract without penalty. Don't waive your right to do your own property inspection, even if your realtor tries to convince you that you could lose the house to another buyer. You need to know what you're getting, especially if you're a first-time buyer.

BRACE YOURSELF FOR THE CLOSING PROCESS

Be prepared for all of the costs associated with the loan, particularly the closing costs. Make sure any online calculators that you use to determine how much house you can afford also take into account attorney's fees, title search, and other one-time fees that you'll have to cough up at closing. These mortgage fees, also called *settlement costs,* cover every expense associated with your loan: inspections, title insurance, taxes, and other charges. Closing costs typically amount to 4% of the sale price.

Rather than use a ballpark percentage, your lender is required by the federal law to provide you with a "good faith estimate" of the fees due at

THE DOWN PAYMENT

For first-time home buyers, often the biggest challenge is coming up with the cash for the down payment. In high-priced areas along the East Coast and in California, sellers can demand as much as 20% of the purchase price as a down payment. Moreover, if your down payment is less than 20%, lenders will require you to pay private mortgage insurance (PMI), an insurance policy that pays the mortgage company if you default on your loan. With prices escalating in some regions, even pulling together 5 or 10% for a down payment can be difficult. But there are some options:

• The Federal Housing Administration (FHA) and Department of Veterans Affairs (VA) guarantee loan programs that are designed to assist first-time home buyers. With an FHA loan, you can buy a house with as little as 3% down, and 100% of the money can be a gift from a relative or a down payment assistance program. The VA loans, which are for active and former members of the United States armed forces, often offer 100% financing—that's no money down! Interest rates on both loans are competitive, and qualifying for them is often easier than qualifying for a loan from a large bank.

• Fannie Mae and Freddie Mac are quasigovernmental agencies that purchase home loans from lenders. If you need a big loan, they can help. In 2007, the maximum loan amount (known as the conforming limit) that these agencies can buy is $417,000 for single-family homes in the United States. They also have other programs for first-time buyers. Fannie Mae has a "Flexible 100," in which borrowers can get up to 100% of the loan amount, and they only need to put $500 down.

closing within three days of your applying for a loan. You can get estimates from several lenders and try to get your favorite lender to meet or beat the best offer, either on the whole package or for specific costs.

The problem is the good faith estimate is still only a "guesstimate" of the final closing costs and the lender is not held responsible if their "estimate" is way off. To prevent any unwanted surprises, it's important to keep close tabs on the process. Property taxes and homeowners insurance are recurring costs that aren't usually open to negotiation. But you may be able to make a deal on one-time costs, such as the real estate attorney's fees, lender's attorney fees, document-preparation fees, the appraisal, and title search. Some lenders offer guaranteed settlement cost packages, which are fixed closing costs, quoted upfront. But you may have to pay a slightly higher rate. Another option: Get the seller to pitch in. If they're eager to sell, you may be able to shift certain closing costs such as the appraisal, underwriting fees, title search, and insurance to the seller and save as much as $8,000.

MOVE-UP BUYERS

Buying your first home is just the warm-up for an exercise that can be even more difficult to juggle: having a home to sell and wanting to purchase another one. In a buyers market, home sellers enjoy the power of choosing among contracts without inspection contingencies. They run the show when it comes to settlement dates and moving. But then the tables are turned, and those "lucky" sellers become buyers, subject to the whims of the people from whom they are purchasing their home.

Call them "move-up buyers" because though some may be downsizing, most are "movin' on up" to a larger, more expensive home. They may be more informed than first-time home buyers: they know the neighborhoods or might already have the names of a few real estate agents. Perhaps the realtor who is selling their current home will find them their new one. Some agents say if you're moving into a more expensive house, then your agent has a big incentive to make sure you sell the house you have and will market it more aggressively.

But after you've found a new home, you still have to figure out how to pay for it. So the same rules apply. Start by getting preapproval for a loan before you start looking for another home—that way you'll know what you can afford. Also ask about various types of loan programs that could get you into a house in the price range that you're thinking about. Hybrid adjustable rate mortgages—where the rate is fixed for the first 3, 5, 7, or 10 years and then adjusts annually—can be significantly cheaper than traditional 30- or 15-year fixed rate loans, which can make a big difference in your monthly payment. Also realize that the key to getting preapproved for a loan for another home depends not only on your credit rating and income, but also on the potential resale value of your current home as well as the equity you have built up.

Agents have differing views on whether you should place your home on the market first or make an offer for your next home. Your answer may depend on how much cash you already have on hand for the purchase, how much you anticipate getting for your current home, and how quickly homes in that price range have sold in your neighborhood. In any case, you need to make sure your finances are in order so that you can make an offer quickly and you also need to prepare your home for sale.

Tip: Make sure when you sell your home that you leave open the possibility of renting back your home after settlement until the new home is ready. To coordinate settlement dates, try to do both closings with the same settlement company.

ARE YOU READY TO SELL?

Paying attention to little details can make a big difference when it comes to getting top dollar for your home. Just a couple hundred dollars and a new coat of paint can make it easily imaginable as a living space for a potential buyer. It doesn't have to mean shelling out $6,000 to construct a deck, $7,000 to put on new siding, or $15,000–$38,000 to add a bathroom—although those

SELLING YOUR HOME

Alisa and her husband, Glenn, thought they had enough experience to sell their Bronxville, New York, home on their own, since they had successfully sold their old house in New Orleans a few years earlier without the help of a broker. "I put a FOR SALE BY OWNER sign and my phone number in the front yard, and by that afternoon, we had phone calls, people coming by," Alisa remembered. The house had sold in a week.

But she knew that in the hypercompetitive New York market, a small sign and word-of-mouth would not be enough to get the $700,000 asking price for her current home. So she took out an ad in the *New York Times* for $1,000, just a fraction of the traditional 6% commission she would probably have to pay a real estate agent. Glenn admitted, "The sole motive for us was to try to save a little bit of money."

That's the primary motivation for most sellers who try to do it on their own. But that also means you are responsible for marketing and advertising the property.

You need to be wary of potential pitfalls too. You could face legal problems if you don't properly handle required disclosures, such as about lead contamination or flooding. Since FSBO sellers don't have to pay commissions, an agent may not be as enthusiastic about showing the house to clients.

An alternative is to pay a flat fee to an Internet service, like ForSale ByOwner.com, or discount broker to list your home on the multiple listing service (MLS), with the understanding that you'll pay a commission to the buyer's agent. Thanks in part to the influx of these Web sites, real estate agents' commissions are coming down. The national average is now closer to 5% and could go even lower, according to a survey by *Real Trends* newsletter.

Even in a hot sellers market, it's not always so easy to make a sale on your own. Alisa and Glenn found the process of closing the deal on their New York home on their own was more stressful than they expected. So they contacted a real estate agent and decided that paying the commission was worth it. The agent closed the deal in a week, finding a buyer who was willing to pay several thousand dollars above their original asking price.

are among the home improvements that have seen the greatest percentage of their costs recovered in recent years. (Go to *www.improvenet.com* to locate a contractor and estimate how much you'll spend to fix up your bathroom, kitchen, and other spaces.)

If you've seen the cable TV show *Designed to Sell,* you know you can make minimal improvements such as fixing tiles in a bathroom, refinishing cabinets, or replacing light fixtures on a budget of $2,000 or less. The more you spend, the more the potential payoff.

First impressions are extremely important, so enhancing curb appeal should be your number one priority. Make sure the lawn and hedges are well manicured. Put a new coat of paint on the house—or at least the trim. You want to draw buyers inside by enticing them from the outside.

With virtual tours and photos of homes available on many real estate Web sites, including *Realtor.com,* it is easier for buyers to envision themselves in the home. But if they are looking on a small screen for the big picture, it is even more important for sellers to keep the interior design simple. Think Pottery Barn—neutral colors, hardwood floors, few personal items—advises realtor Susan Law. The pictures and special collections need to be put away. Remember you're selling the house, not your home.

TAPPING THE VALUE IN YOUR HOME

For some couples, their house is like a money tree, and they'd like to shake it to pay for everything from their children's college tuition to a new car. When home prices were rising a few years ago and interest rates were at record lows, millions of homeowners tapped the equity in their homes in the form of a cash-out refinancing, home equity loans, or lines of credit. Using your house as a piggy bank may seem like a smart way to get cash, but if you're not careful it could wind up costing you more than you think.

CASH-OUT REFINANCING

When it was time to refinance the loan on her suburban Philadelphia home, Amy went on the Internet and started to call banks and credit unions to compare rates on 30-year and 15-year mortgages. She found the interest rate and type of loan she wanted online at a national lender and refinanced twice in two years. "If you just ask the right questions, you can usually get exactly what you want," Amy says. Refinancing your primary mortgage lets you borrow more than you currently owe on your home, so you can pocket the difference. In a low-interest-rate environment, you probably won't see that much of an increase in your monthly payments. But remember, you'll stretch out your loan term, which means you'll ultimately be paying more. A low rate may be tied to hefty costs, so make sure you find out upfront what all the expenses

---

 AVOID BEING LOCKED OUT

In a rising rate environment, it's especially important to lock in the lowest-possible rate in a timely manner. A few years ago, Melissa, a financial adviser in New York, watched the interest on a 15-year fixed rate mortgage for her Manhattan apartment shoot up from 5 to 6% in a matter of days. Although she initially locked in the lower rate, a delay in the processing of her application could have meant missing an important deadline and getting stuck with the higher prevailing rate and a bigger monthly mortgage payment.

The best way for home buyers and refinancers to cushion themselves against rate shock during closing is by signing, as Melissa did, an agreement—called a "lock in" agreement—with lenders that guarantees a specific rate for 30, 45, or 60 days. The problem is a lock in can be canceled if the loan processing isn't completed by the time an agreement expires. So keep track of that expiration date. For Melissa, frequent calls to her loan officer helped her close on time at the 5% rate.

associated with the loan will be. These should be included in a document known as a "good faith estimate." Find out about hidden penalties as well; some lenders will hit you with a fee if you refinance before a certain date. Knowing that in advance helped Annette save thousands with her refinancing.

Tip: You may be able to lower your mortgage payments without refinancing. "Loan modification" lets you lower the rate on your existing mortgage without paying closing costs and other fees, which can total up to 3% of the loan amount. Not all banks offer it—and those that do, don't advertise—but it certainly doesn't hurt to ask.

HOME EQUITY LOANS AND LINES OF CREDIT

Whether they're paying for college, buying a new car, or paying off credit cards, more and more consumers are borrowing against their homes to get the cash. Home equity loans, particularly lines of credit, make good sense for a lot of people. Home equity loans are like a second mortgage. They are made in a lump sum at fixed interest rates. Lines of credit are open-ended and rates, which adjust monthly, are tied to the prime rate. Among the advantages of both: rates are far lower than what you'd pay on a credit card, an extended payment period (5 to 20 years) can help you manage cash flow, and interest payments on the first $100,000 are tax-deductible. (Although if you're subject to the alternative minimum tax, interest is deductible only if the loan is used for home improvements.) Plus, some lines of credit can be obtained with no upfront fees.

My husband, Chris, and I didn't move from New York City to a house in the suburbs on a whim. We weren't sure what kind of "culture shock" we would experience, if any at all. So we found a "huge" apartment—well, it was huge to us considering it was about three times as big as our Manhattan digs—in Westchester County, New York. We thought that would be a good way to get used to the suburbs and explore that city and neighboring towns. Our home "exploration" expedition took three years! It also took us that

DECIDING BETWEEN A HOME EQUITY LOAN AND LINE OF CREDIT

• Go for a line of credit if you're not sure how much, or even if, you need to borrow.

• Go for a line of credit if you can repay the loan in four years or less. Get a home equity loan if it will take you longer than four years to repay.

• Choose a home equity loan if you think you may borrow too much from a line of credit.

For many borrowers, consolidating debt with a home equity loan or line of credit seems like a good way to get some breathing room. Most couples will use the loans to pay for home renovations, some use it to jump-start business ventures, while others will pay off debts. The problem is when interest rates rise, some people may find themselves unable to cover the loan. Says Bankrate.com's senior financial analyst Greg McBride: "All the jockeying around that people do to consolidate debt at lower interest rates is great, but that is really only the first step. The second step is actually repaying that debt and that's best done when interest rates are low rather than when they move higher." Remember, credit card companies can't foreclose on your house if you run into financial problems, but you could lose your home if you default on a home equity loan or line of credit!

amount of time to save enough money for a down payment. We could have rushed it and bought the first three-bedroom one-story ranch house that we saw. It was beautifully decorated and had all new bathrooms—but the roof needed to be replaced (a $7,000 expense!). Instead, we waited and we found our ideal home, a 1920s Tudor that we have no intention of leaving for decades to come. Bottom line: Don't rush to buy (or sell).

5

COLLEGE SAVINGS 101
Send Your Kid to College Without Going Broke.

There are as many ways of saving for higher education as there are majors at college. Here are a few of them:

The Head-Starters. Three-year old Jake is lucky his mom is in the financial planning business. Melissa, a New York City financial adviser, and her husband set up a 529 college savings account for Jake two weeks after he was born, which has since grown. With tuition costs skyrocketing to more than $10,000 a year for the average public college and over $25,000 for the average private university, Melissa and her husband have calculated that sending little Jake to an Ivy League school in 2020 will cost well over six-figures in today's dollars. Earnings and withdrawals on state-sponsored 529 college savings plans are completely tax-free, making 529 plans a very smart choice.

The Shifters. Donald and Pamela didn't waste any time starting a college fund for their two children either. A few months after the birth of their first child, Rachel, the couple invested $15,000 for her in a custodial account. They deposited the same amount in a similar account when their son, Don, was born. For Rachel, now 15, and Don, now 12, the bull market resulted in big returns in their accounts in the late 1990s. But when the market started to head south, Donald and Pamela weren't sure their college savings would weather the market's downturn and still cover rising tuition bills. In 2003, the Florida couple decided to take $13,000 out of each child's stash to buy contracts in the state's prepaid tuition plan, a program designed to cover four years of *future* tuition and dorm expenses in *today's* dollars. Donald and Pamela didn't expect to qualify for financial aid, so they looked for other college savings vehicles with even better tax breaks. Income limits have prevented them from contributing to a Coverdell Education Savings Account, a tax-deferred college savings option. So, their next step was to move the bulk of college money from the custodial accounts into state-sponsored 529 college savings plans for more tax-advantaged growth.

The Borrowers. Joe and Pam were thrilled when their oldest son earned an academic scholarship for college, but they knew that sum would make only a small dent in his $26,000-a-year tuition bill. Joe and Pam agreed that Delaware Valley College was a good fit for Joe Jr. but it cost a lot more than they'd planned, and they wondered how they would swing it. Joe, an accounting manager, and Pam, a stay-at-home mom, didn't qualify for financial aid, but they've since managed to cover his college costs with a combination of federal and state loans.

You don't need a college degree to realize that college costs are very high. Harvard, for example, charged $43,655 in tuition, room, board, and fees last year—which was only a shade less than the U.S. median household income in 2005, of $46,326, according to the Census Bureau. As much as parents may wish they could foot the entire bill for higher education for their children, the rising cost of campus life could make that impossible. Ideally, when a couple decides they want to have children, they should start putting money in some type of college fund, preferably one that offers some tax advantages. You can even open the account before the child is born. It's even a wise idea to start when you begin *trying* to have a baby—if things don't work out, and one hopes that they do, you can always use the money for a vacation, or for adult education of your own. Soon after I learned I was pregnant with our first child, I opened a 529 college savings plan, naming myself as the beneficiary, and made my first deposit. Then I changed the beneficiary to my son a few weeks after he was born, and we now contribute to our daughter's college savings in another account as well. (Each year, my husband and I each try to contribute $5,000 to their college savings. We don't always reach that goal, but we try. New York state offers residents a tax break on 529 plan contributions. The maximum state tax deduction for a couple in New York is $10,000.) Most parents don't begin saving for college that soon—or that regularly. According to a 2004 survey by American Century Investments, almost two-thirds (63%) of parents fear they are not saving enough for their children's education and are concerned about their children having to go into debt to pay for postsecondary education.

Many families will still have to take out federal and/or private loans to supplement their college savings, if they've been disciplined enough to save at all. Luckily there is plenty of money for couples to borrow. This chapter helps couples understand what is available, in terms of savings vehicles as well as financial aid resources.

CRASH COURSE ON COLLEGE SAVINGS PLANS

When it comes to saving for college or any other financial goal, the first step is determining how much money you will need. Don't plan on your kid going to state college, or not going to college at all. That could possibly put you in the uncomfortable position of hoping junior doesn't get into, say, Columbia or Stanford—simply because you can't afford it. That won't get you into the Parenting Hall of Fame. You also shouldn't count on your child winning a scholarship. It's a laudable goal and one that should be pursued—but not something you should depend on.

Figure out what you're getting into. Many brokerage houses, banks, and other financial Web sites offer online college cost predictors. T. Rowe Price's Web site (*www.troweprice.com*) offers a very clear breakdown of how much money you need to save each year for your child or children based on projected tuition at major colleges and universities in the United States, and on the investment return and rate of inflation you chose.

Using the calculator, we figured out it will cost more than $1 million to send our four-year-old son and one-year-old daughter to Harvard! That's provided college costs don't rise more than 7% a year. We could get depressed by those numbers, but we won't. Knowing the amount that we ultimately need to save has helped us figure out the best approach in terms of the plans we've chosen and how we've decided to allocate our investments.

To help you figure out a college savings strategy for your family, you first need to know what options are available. No matter which path you take, the key to building a college fund is to start saving as early as possible and put money in regularly. But don't make the mistake that financial advisers tell me they see all too often. Many people dump huge sums of money into college savings and neglect retirement. Remember, there's always a chance you can get grants and loans for college, but not for retirement. The Bill and Melinda Gates Foundation isn't going to pick up the tab for your condo in Florida. Now, here's a crash course on the college savings options that are available.

529 COLLEGE SAVINGS PLANS

The best chance at saving the most money for your child's college costs is probably a state-sponsored 529 plan, usually categorized as a prepaid or savings plan (we'll get to 529 prepaid plans in a moment). The 529 college savings plan allows your earnings to grow tax-free and doesn't make you pay taxes when you take the money out. These are the only college savings programs that are completely sheltered from federal taxes (many states offer a tax deduction, too), plus they have no income restrictions. Over the past few years, parents have stashed billions into these plans. Some projections see assets hitting the $200 billion mark in the next five years. Still, these plans might not be right for everyone. Here are some of the pros and cons:

Pros

- Nearly every state has a 529 plan, sponsored by the state and managed by a financial services firm, such as Vanguard, Merrill Lynch, or T. Rowe Price.
- Contributions grow federally tax-free and you pay no federal income tax on withdrawals.
- You can contribute up to $60,000 all at once (or $120,000 for a married couple) without paying gift taxes. However, you wouldn't be able to make another contribution for the next five years.
- Funds in 529 plans can be used for tuition, fees, room, board, books, supplies, and other equipment.
- Many states also offer a state tax deduction on contributions. Some set a cap at $2,500. Other states (such as South Carolina, West Virginia, Colorado, and New Mexico) are especially generous, allowing you to deduct every penny you put in. That may be a good reason to invest in your own state's plan. Most states that allow deductions for contributions require that you invest in their plan to receive the benefit. However, that is no longer the case in Pennsylvania and as of 2007 is not the case in Maine and Kansas. Residents in those states can invest in just about any state's plan and still receive the tax deduction from their home state.
- In a few states (Michigan, Minnesota, and Louisiana), you'll get free money for participating in the plan if your income is below a certain level. Similar to the "match" that many employers deposit into their workers' 401(k) accounts, these states basically *pay you* for putting money in. Michigan will match your first $200 in contributions, while Minnesota will chip in with up to $300 a year for families who qualify. In Louisiana, depending on how much money you make, the state will provide a match of up to 14% of your contributions. (The minimum is

currently 2%, so even the state's high-income earners can participate in at least a portion of the state's match game.)

- You can contribute as much money as you want each year, up to the lifetime limit, which varies by state. For example, in Pennsylvania, the overall limit is $315,000 per beneficiary, and the maximum is $235,000 in New York. But you could contribute that amount in one lump sum the first year.

- Minimum investments typically range from $250 to $1,000, but you can sock away as little as $25 a month through an automatic investment program. (New York's plan lets you start putting away just $15 a month, if you sign up through a payroll deduction plan.)

- You can invest in just about any state's plan, no matter where you live, and the beneficiary can use the money to attend any college or university in the country.

- You can name any child, anyone, even yourself, as the beneficiary. If your first child decides not to go to college or doesn't use all of the money, you can transfer the funds to the second child.

- A new law enacted in 2006 prevents a 529 college savings account (or prepaid tuition plan) from being assessed at the high rate (20% for the 2007–08 academic year) applied to most student-owned assets. Instead, the 529 will be counted at no more than the 5.64% rate for parent-owned assets. And it may not be counted at all, depending on how the new law is interpreted by the U.S. Department of Education.

Cons

- If you dip into the college coffers for other expenses, you'll be slapped with a 10% penalty on withdrawn earnings and have to pay federal income taxes to boot.

- You can't select your own investments. You're stuck with the plan's various asset allocation models. Some states offer 3 or 4, some 20 or more. Age-based portfolios in a fund that shifts from stocks to bonds as the child gets closer to college are probably best for most parents who are afraid of too much risk. You can also move your money between portfolios (though you are limited to one change per year). And you can transfer funds to a different 529 plan as often as once every twelve months (though read the plan's prospectus carefully before you do to ensure you aren't hit with unnecessary charges).

- You are at the whim of the state and federal government as well as plan sponsors, who can make changes to the plan at any time. A few years ago, I was stunned to find out that all of the funds in my son's 529 plan would be automatically transferred from TIAA-CREF to new investments offered by Vanguard, when the state switched to a Vanguard-run 529 plan. If I didn't like the Vanguard plan, my only options were to transfer my funds to a New York State 529 plan offered only by financial advisers and brokers or switch to an out-of-state plan. Luckily, I like Vanguard funds.

- Your account balance can get severely beaten down with fees. All 529 plans charge a management fee that typically ranges from about, 0.25 to 0.70% a year, but some plans will also hit you with an enrollment charge, annual maintenance fee, and annual expenses charged by the underlying mutual funds in your portfolio—which can be as high as 2.4%. (You can find your state's fees at *www.savingforcollege.com*.) Nebraska and Wisconsin sponsor some of the most expensive plans. Fees in some states may outweigh the tax advantages and even low-fee plans may not be worth it if you buy them through brokers who charge commissions as high as 5.75%.

- The money must be used for college. There is a 10% penalty on earnings for nonqualified distributions (except if you terminate the account because the beneficiary has died or is disabled), or if you withdraw funds that aren't needed because your child gets a scholarship—you can always change the beneficiary to a sibling to keep the account going.

529 Plan Checklist. Overall, the positive aspects of 529 plans outweigh the negative ones. However, since the situation of each couple and family is unique, these plans are certainly not right for everyone. Keep in mind that just because you're investing in a 529 plan or another type of account doesn't necessarily mean your child's tuition is covered. You need to understand there are always inherent risks in investing. Even if you start saving for your newborn's education now, if the stock market takes some big dips and the account is mostly invested in stocks, you may not have an adequate sum when you're ready to use those funds for college. Still, it's better to invest for college—and be able to cover at least some of the costs—than to save nothing at all. Here are some questions you may want to ask before choosing a 529 plan:

- Who is the fund manager?
- Does the plan offer a variety of mutual funds, including fixed income investments?

 SAVE FOR COLLEGE BY SPENDING

A few Web sites, like Upromise, BabyMint and LittleGrad, will automatically send a percentage of your purchases to a college savings account whenever you shop at a participating retailer, sign up for services with participating providers, register your phone number, or use a designated credit card. Each plan has different variations on the opportunities for earning rebates. Friends, grandparents, anyone, can sign up and direct the rewards to your college savings account. Then most of these sites will let you automatically deposit your rebate rewards into 529 plans. But there is a catch. Shopping more doesn't necessarily mean that you'll save more. These sites may have a contribution limit. At Upromise, the maximum you can contribute is $300 a year. Check out *www.upromise.com, www.babymint.com,* and *www.littlegrad.com.*

- Does the plan impose any harsh restrictions? For example, New York penalizes investors who wish to later roll over their funds to another state's plan.
- Is it favorable toward nonresidents?
- Can you buy the plan directly from the state or plan sponsor, or do you have to go through a broker-dealer?
- Does your state offer any additional tax advantages?

PREPAID TUITION PLANS

A 529 prepaid plan promises to pay for tomorrow's tuition by locking in today's rates, plus it offers some of the same tax breaks as 529 college savings plans. Your state may offer a 529 college savings or 529 prepaid plan or both. Colleges and universities can also offer 529 prepaid plans, but not a 529 college savings plan. Withdrawals are also tax-free when used for college expenses, but usually cover only tuition and fees. Some prepaid plans let you prepay for a certain number of courses your child will take in the future. Others allow you to prepay an entire year's worth of tuition and fees. If you are in a program that sells tuition units or credits, you may not be protected from future price hikes. Locking in a full-year (or better yet, four-year) tuition contract is much safer. In most states, the beneficiary of the prepaid plan must be a state resident. In some states, the account owner must also live in-state.

With college costs creeping up twice as fast as inflation, a 529 prepaid plan could be a great deal. But again, these plans aren't for everyone. Prepaid plans are best for families who want conservative investments.

- You'd probably wind up with more money if you invested in a 529 college savings plan's portfolio that included stocks.
- You should also understand the risks. This type of guarantee can cost you. Thanks to the stock market's volatility and rising college

INDEPENDENT 529 PLAN

A recent twist on the prepaid plan is the Independent 529 Plan, which allows parents to prepay a child's private college tuition for one of more than 250 participating schools (including Amherst, Stanford, Notre Dame, and Princeton) at a discount to today's rates. You can buy certificates that represent a different percentage of tuition at each school. The Independent 529 Plan is probably best suited for couples who fall into these three categories: conservative investors, parents and students who favor private colleges, and universities and alumni of private schools who would like to see their children attend their alma maters.

Now investing in the Independent 529 Plan won't guarantee that your child will get into Princeton, Oberlin, or one of the other member colleges and who knows if your kid will even want to go to one of those schools. However, refunds are available—capped at plus or minus 2% based on fund performance—and parents can roll over the money without penalty to another beneficiary or regular college savings plan or state prepaid plan.

To keep your options open, you may want to invest in an Independent 529 Plan and your own state's prepaid plan. But since these plans usually only cover tuition and fees, not room and board, you also may want to put away some money in a 529 college savings plan (which covers tuition, fees, room and board, and can also be used to pay for graduate school) and even a Coverdell account (to take care of secondary school expenses, like private school or SAT prep courses, before you child even reaches the campus).

costs, many prepaid plans have experienced some financial troubles. Some plans are now charging a premium on today's tuition prices for letting you lock in the lower rates. Several have closed to new investors.

Finally, what happens if your kid decides not to go to a school that's covered under the prepaid plan or decides not to go to college at all? You can change the beneficiary and earmark the funds for another child. If that is not an option, state-run plans usually figure out how much tuition your investment would buy, on average, at an in-state school and will give you that refund in cash, minus any administrative fees. The private plan refunds an amount equal to your original investment, adjusted by the performance—which is usually limited to a maximum annualized gain or loss of 2%.

The most comprehensive source of information on 529 college savings plans and prepaid plans can be found at *www.savingforcollege.com*. Each state's plan is reviewed, including investment options, administrative costs, and contribution limits. Joseph Hurley, who started and manages this site, has a book: *The Best Way to Save for College: A Complete Guide to 529 Plans.* Also check out the College Saving Plans Network at *www.collegesavings.org*, an affiliate of the National Association of State Treasurers, that can link you to a particular state plan's Web site.

COVERDELL EDUCATION SAVINGS ACCOUNTS

Formerly known as Education IRAs, Coverdell Education Savings Accounts also have tax advantages and are more flexible than 529 plans. You can also choose and control your own investments, just as in a traditional or Roth IRA. Funds in Coverdell accounts can be used to cover *all* education costs— not only college expenses, but also private elementary or high school and other "educational" expenses, like a new computer and even camp (although that Kindergarten–12th grade provision is set to expire in 2010). And, like 529 college savings plans, no more than 5.6% of your savings will go into your expected family contribution for financial aid calculations.

But there are limits to how much you can save and who can participate. Contributions are limited to $2,000 a year per student (no matter how many people contribute to the account) and limits who can participate. Full contributions start to phase out for married couples with adjusted gross incomes over $190,000. Couples who make over $220,000 can't contribute at all. There are ways around that, though: If your child already earns some income and will file a tax return, give $2,000 to your child (or have them use their own earnings) to contribute to the account. Or ask Grandma and Grandpa to fund it, if their income is below the threshold.

It's a great way to save, if you can only put away a little bit at a time and have a long time to save, or if you're saving in a Coverdell and a second account. Many advisers suggest putting the first $2,000 a year that you've allotted for college savings in a Coverdell, then fund a 529 plan.

ROTH IRA

This type of individual retirement account (IRA) may also be an attractive option for college savings. Since many couples are saving for college and retirement at the same time, consider contributing to a Coverdell and a Roth IRA. The Roth IRA is an individual retirement account but offers a huge benefit to those who may need to spend some of those savings before they actually retire. A Roth IRA must be established for at least five years and the account holder has to be at least 59½ before any qualified withdrawal of *earnings* can be made tax-free, in this case for specific higher education expenses. Otherwise, the withdrawal will be subject to income tax on the *earnings.* Since retirement funds usually aren't counted in financial aid formulas, many financial planners say the Roth IRA is a very attractive option, particularly for parents with younger children.

The Roth lets you take out contributions at any time, tax- and penalty-free, so you can tap the money for college expenses if you don't hang onto it for retirement. Roth IRAs allow a husband and wife to each contribute up to $4,000 a year—for a total of $8,000 annually (plus an extra $1,000 each, if age 50 or older)—and take out up to half of the balance for college expenses. Starting in 2008, the annual contribution limit increases to $5,000 a year, or $10,000 for a couple. However, a married couple filing jointly must have an adjusted gross income of less than $166,000 to be eligible to contribute.

CUSTODIAL ACCOUNTS

For wealthy couples who want greater control over where their investment dollars will go, custodial accounts may be a better bet. With low tax rates in place at least until 2010, Uniform Transfers to Minors Act (UTMA) accounts and Uniform Gift to Minors Accounts (UGMA) may be a sensible alternative to 529 plans or Coverdell accounts. You can each contribute up to $12,000 a year without paying gift taxes. If your child is under 14, the first $850 of annual earnings is tax-free, so that could be a good place to park the money your child receives on birthdays and other special occasions throughout the year. The second $850 is taxed at the child's rate of 10% (5% for dividends and capital gains) and anything above $1,700 is taxed at the parent's higher tax rate— probably 15% on dividends and long-term capital gains. For children over age 17, earnings on investments after the first $850 are taxed at their own rate.

The good news is there's no penalty if the money isn't used for college. But that could turn out to be bad news if your kid decides to hike in the Himalayas instead of heading to Harvard. At a certain age (21 in most states and 18 in a few), your child gets control of the dough and can use it for *anything*. Also, if you think your family may qualify for financial aid, remember UTMA and UGMA accounts are considered student assets, assessed at a 20% rate for the 2007–08 academic year.

SAVE IN YOUR OWN NAME

With dividends and long-term capital gains taxed at just 15%, it may make sense to stash at least some of your child's college savings in your own

COMPARING COLLEGE PLANS

PLAN	TAX STATUS	ADVANTAGES	DISADVANTAGES
529 Plan	Tax-free*	Some states offer extra tax breaks.	Fees can be high.
Coverdell Account	Tax-free*	Huge number of investment choices.	Contributions capped at $2,000 a year.
Roth IRA	Contributions are tax-free.	Can withdraw money tax-free.	Don't want to eat up your retirement savings.
Custodial Account	First $850 in investment income each year is tax-free. Next $850 taxed at child's rate.	Huge number of investment choices. Children 14 and older pay tax at their own rate on gains above $1,700.	Investment income above $1,700 a year is taxed at parent's top rate if child is younger than 14.

*If used for higher education expenses.

name. Look for tax-efficient investments, like a stock index fund or an exchange-traded fund. When you sell the investment, you may want to gift some of the money to your child to take advantage of the lower taxes on gains. But then again, if you kept the money in your name, even though you'd wind up paying 15% on long-term capital gains, the money would be counted as a parental asset—and therefore reduce the expected family contribution—according to financial aid calculations. If you have big losses from your investments, you may be able to book those losses against gains to equal tax-free withdrawals with no penalties even if your child decides not to go to college.

If you want maximum control over your investments, keeping college funds in a brokerage account in your name is the way to go. There are no rules as to how you invest the money, how often you make changes to your account, or how you spend the money. If your child decides not to go to college, you can use it for that Alaskan cruise you always wanted to take.

The downside: taxable accounts can't come close to the compounded returns of tax-free 529 plans. The mutual fund company T. Rowe Price found that no matter where you live, if you were to invest $5,000 a year for a child in a 529 plan starting at age 10, on average, your money would grow to $62,850 in an out-of-state 529 plan (not your state's plan) by the time he or she hits 18, assuming an 8% annual gain. (You'd earn $64,428, about $1,500 more in your state's plan (if, for example, it offered a $1,000 state tax deduction annually.) That same amount invested similarly in a regular brokerage account would come to $58,641 after taxes. So if you decide to keep college funds in your own name, stick with low-cost, tax-efficient mutual funds.

STRATEGIES TO MAXIMIZE YOUR COLLEGE SAVINGS

No college savings vehicle is perfect for each and every family. But you can probably figure out a strategy that will work for you by focusing on four factors: your tax bracket, your child's age, how much control you want over your investments, and how much financial aid you expect to get. Use your income and tax bracket as a guide, provided tax laws pretty much stay the same until your kids are out of college. If the tax law changes, you'll need to revisit your strategy. Here are some possible strategies for couples based on your current household income. In each case you'll be able to either maximize your financial aid package or enhance your tax savings—but it's usually tough to do both.

YOUR INCOME: UNDER $64,000
YOUR GOAL: MAXIMIZE YOUR FINANCIAL AID

Lower-income couples who fall in the 10 to 15% tax brackets, with taxable incomes under $63,700, for married filing jointly, don't really benefit all that much from tax-deferred accounts, like 529 plans and Coverdell accounts. Your taxes are pretty low already and since you probably have the best shot at getting financial aid, you want to make sure you don't hurt your chances by contributing to a custodial (UTMA, UGMA) account.

Best bet: Keep savings in your own name. Parental assets count less than student assets in financial aid calculations. Generally, you'll only pay 5% on capital gains and dividends (instead of the usual 15%) and you'll have the flexibility to use the money any way you want. Seek out low-cost index funds, such as those offered by Vanguard or Fidelity. Also, since retirement savings and home equity generally aren't counted in financial aid formulas, save the max in your retirement accounts and keep up your mortgage payments.

YOUR INCOME:$64,000 TO $196,000
YOUR GOAL: STAY FLEXIBLE

Middle-income couples in the 25% bracket with taxable income below $128,500 may still be eligible for financial aid. (Though, keep in mind, 60% of most aid packages are loans, not grants or scholarships.) Since you'll probably have to chip in some money, you'll probably want to take advantage of tax-deferred accounts. But, remember, you can't claim valuable tax credits, such as the Hope or Lifetime Learning credit, for college expenses you pay with 529 plan funds. (If your joint income is over $94,000, you may not qualify for these credits anyway.)

Even upper-middle-income couples in the 28% bracket, with taxable income up to $195,850 for married couples filing jointly, may be lucky enough to get financial aid. Although "aid" often consists largely of loans, maybe your child will earn a merit scholarship. Still, you probably will have to come up with the bulk of the tab.

Best bets: Coverdell accounts, Roth IRAs, 529 plans, tax-efficient investments in your own name. Stash your first $2,000 in a Coverdell (you can choose any low-cost fund) and put the rest in a 529 savings plan. Unless you receive a sizable state tax deduction, you'll probably come out further ahead if you simply choose the lowest-cost plan, especially if you're investing a large lump sum.

And buy some savings bonds for safety. When stocks are strong, the returns will be far lower than most 529 plan portfolios, but you may get a tax break. The interest on savings bonds also may be tax free if the money is used for tuition or fees. Go to the U.S. Treasury's Web site, *www.savingsbond.gov,* for more details.

YOUR INCOME: OVER $196,000
YOUR GOAL: FOCUS ON TAX-FREE SAVINGS

Finally for the well-to-do in the top two brackets (33% if your adjusted gross income is up to $349,700, 35% if it's over that), the strategy is pretty simple. Since you already know you'll be footing the bill, your goal is to minimize your tax bite. You'll get a great tax break, plus estate planning perks.

Best bet: Definitely invest in 529s. Money contributed to a 529 plan is considered a complete gift, so you don't have to worry about paying taxes on the account if anything happens to you. However, if you want more choice in your investments, UTMAs and UGMAs will give you more control.

For a quick check to see which college savings option may be best for you, use the College Savings Options tool on Vanguard's Web site. T. Rowe Price and Fidelity also have useful tools on their sites.

KIDS CAN CHIP IN TOO

College costs shouldn't be only the parents' concern. Children can help out too—starting with keeping their grades up. Students who place in the top 20% of their class are sought after by schools and are often eligible for scholarships and grants. Also, if your child takes enough advanced placement (AP) courses in high school and scores well on the AP exam, he or she may be able to enter college as a second-semester freshman or even sophomore. Teach them to save and invest by encouraging them to set aside money for college as well. For every $25 your middle school or high school student puts in from babysitting or mowing the lawn, you can put in an equal amount. Once they're in college, they can work 10–20 hours a week at an off-campus or, if eligible, work-study job to pay for personal expenses. Some financial aid counselors say students who hold part-time jobs actually have better graduation rates. Finally, students need to know how to manage their money before they leave home. Parents should take notes, too.)

• *Make sure they understand credit.* If your child has a credit card, make sure they know how it works. You may want to try a starter card—a prepaid, reloadable card that's limited to $1,000.

• *Create a spending plan* so that your child knows how much they can spend each month on food, books, and entertainment, and what their spending allowance will be.

• *Don't automatically bail them out:* Your first reaction may be to send your child money as soon as they ask for it or get into a financial bind. But if you start, you may not be able to stop. So let your child know they'll have to get a job or work more hours if they spend more money than they are allotted for the month.

BEST INVESTMENTS FOR YOUR CHILD'S AGE

The most successful way to save for college or any other financial goal is to make it part of your budget. Once you've chosen the type of investment vehicle you want to use, contribute the same amount to that fund each month—that's known as dollar-cost averaging. By using that method, the cost of the stock, mutual fund, or bond fund will average out to be less than a one-time lump sum investment.

The key is choosing the right type of investment. Just like saving for retirement or some other financial goal, how you decide to allocate your college savings among stocks, bonds, and cash or other short-term reserves will depend on whether you are an aggressive, moderate, or conservative investor and how long you have to invest.

If you are a middle-of-the-road type who doesn't mind taking on a little risk, but not too much, in order to get medium-size returns, you'll probably start out overweighting your portfolio with stocks when your child is younger and then gradually increase the bond portion as your son or daughter gets closer to college age. According to Vanguard, historically, a portfolio like this earned average returns of 7 to 9.7% from 1960 to 2003, with the highest gains in the years that were heavily invested in stocks. Aggressive investors may tilt their asset allocation more heavily toward stocks early on and conservative investors would split the difference more evenly.

OTHER PEOPLE'S MONEY: FINANCIAL AID

Contributing to any college savings plan will put you well on your way to empowering your child with the higher education he or she will need to enhance their future. Still, you need to be realistic. You simply may not be able to save enough money to foot your child's entire college tab. But there are other options. Don't assume your six-figure salary is a signal to financial aid officers that your family should not receive any aid. More than 20% of students with household incomes over $100,000 receive need-based financial

HIDDEN COSTS OF COLLEGE

Unexpected expenses—travel, phone calls, computers, club memberships, fees and permits—can add thousands to the cost of your child's education. Then, there are those expenses that creep up on you even before they set foot on campus. Dina and Howard found the process of helping their oldest son, Daniel, get into one of his top college choices cost them almost half the full price at the average private university. A year of SAT prep courses: $7,000. Private financial aid counselor: $2,000. Airfare and hotels to visit five colleges and universities: $2,000. Application fees: $500. Total: $11,500. To avoid busting your college savings budget before your child even gets there, lean on your high school guidance counselor, instead of hiring an outside expert. Sometimes the best way to find out about what type of aid may be available to your child is to contact the college financial aid office directly. Also check out some of the free online test preparation services, such as www.number2.com or have your child review sample tests provided through the College Board (www.collegeboard.com). Many college Web sites offer video tours of the campus, or you can buy your own videotape. For $15, you can get a grainy, home-movie-like videotape of one of more than 350 colleges from Collegiate Choice Walking Tours Video (www.collegiatechoice.com). And since books are often one of the most variable and unpredictable expenses, tell Junior to check the prices on eBay (www.ebay.com) as well as online discount book stores (www.bestbookbuys.com, www.varsitybooks.com, www.bigwords.com) before heading to the campus bookstore. One of the biggest fees can be the health services fee that many schools charge. But most full-time students are covered under their parents' health plan until they're 23 years old. So get that fee waived if your child is covered under your policy.

aid. When it comes to acing Financial Aid 101, the trick is figuring out what aid you're eligible for—then getting it. You may be more likely to qualify for aid if your annual income is less than $70,000, but many schools will offer some aid to talented students whose parents earn more. Loans make up about 60% of financial aid—the rest is "free money" in the form of scholarships and grants. Use the tools at *www.collegeboard.com* or *www.finaid.org* to calculate your expected family contribution and figure out whether you have a chance of getting help.

FILLING OUT THE FORMS

Federal and state aid is awarded based on the information on a student's Free Application for Federal Student Aid (FAFSA). (You can complete the form online at *www.fafsa.ed.gov*.) Fill it out and send it in close to January 1 of the year in which you will be enrolled. The U.S. Education Department operates a free hotline (800-4-FED-AID) for questions involving federal student aid. Public colleges follow the forms pretty closely, and private schools also factor it into their offers. The College Scholarship Service Profile is another form used by hundreds of schools and many organizations that offer scholarships. Most people don't submit that form until the fall of the student's senior year of high school, long after the FAFSA, because you must indicate the schools to which you're applying. (Find the CSSP on the *www.collegeboard.com*.) You need to complete both forms every year that you apply for aid. You'll need to refer to tax forms, pay stubs, and brokerage and bank account statements, so make sure you have them handy. (After you file your taxes in April, you can append your FAFSA form. Also, if you have a change in your family situation—divorce, death, or loss of job, for example—it's important to update the form.) Once a college has your FAFSA, it calculates eligibility by taking the cost of attending a particular college minus the expected family contribution (EFC). The EFC is based largely on income, but is also affected by your assets, the number of children you have attending college at the same time, and the number of years you have until retirement.

The federal government's formula for determining your EFC weighs your assets and number of dependents currently in college, in addition to income. When it comes to assets, those in the parents' name are assessed at 5–6%. Student assets are assessed at 20% starting in 2007, income at 50%. The difference between the expected family contribution and the actual cost is your financial need. As a result, nearly all families could qualify for some form of financial aid.

The institutional method used by most private schools is slightly more complicated than the federal formula. It makes allowances for such things as emergency savings and money put aside for younger children. Private schools are also often more willing to look beyond the numbers and take other situations into account, such as a sibling with a chronic illness or a particularly high cost of living.

Aid offers should start arriving in your mailbox around the same time your child receives an acceptance letter from the school. You may see differences in aid offers from different schools. Aid packages vary not only in how much aid is offered, but how it is divided into grants and loans. You may be able to discuss your aid package with financial aid officers and appeal your case. They may be able to match or at least come closer to your best aid offer. (The College Board site, *www.collegeboard.com*, has an excellent worksheet for comparing offers.)

GRANTS

The best packages are made up by grants, which are categorized as need-based, merit-based, federal, state, and institutional. Grants are usually tax-free and don't have to be repaid. The largest federal grant programs, the Pell Grant and the federal Supplemental Educational Opportunity Grants, are based strictly on need and are generally nonnegotiable. Pell Grants, which usually go to students from low-income families, offer a maximum of $4,000 for the 2006–07 award year (July 1, 2006–June 30, 2007). The maximum can change each award year depending on program finding. SEOP grants range from $100 to $4,000 a year. Grants that come directly from a school are often a mix of need-based and merit-based, which can be based on anything from academics to ethnicity to athletics. "But even wealthy students on some college campuses will get institutional aid, which is basically a discount on the sticker price of the cost of college," says Michael O'Brien, CEO of *EDLOAN.com,* an online education finance company. Many colleges also offer what is known as "retention grants" to students with high academic performance after they have been enrolled for a year or more in order to keep them at the school.

Two new grants became available in the 2006–07 school year. The first is an Academic Competitiveness Grant providing up to $750 for the first year of undergraduate study and $1,300 for the second year of undergraduate study to full-time students who are U.S. citizens, eligible for a Pell Grant, and who had completed a rigorous high school program. The second is a National SMART Grant providing up to $4,000 for each of the third and fourth years of undergraduate study to full-time students who are U.S. citizens, eligible for the Pell Grant, and majoring in sciences, mathematics, technology, engineering, or a foreign language critical to national security.

LOANS FOR STUDENTS

The bulk of student aid comes in the form of subsidized and unsubsidized loans. *Subsidized loans* typically carry low interest rates and don't have to be repaid until several months after the student has graduated. With the federal *Perkins loan,* students can borrow up to $4,000 a year for five years at a very low interest rate, usually 5%. The total you can borrow as an undergradutate is $20,000, but it is up to a particular college to determine the size of a specific student's loan. As of July 1, 2006, there were several changes to student loans that increased rates for most borrowers—but they're still relatively low. The *Stafford loan* now has a fixed interest rate of 6.8% for new loans. Students may borrow up to maximums that rise the longer a student remains in school, from $3,500 in the first year to $5,500 in the senior year. Undergraduates can borrow a maximum of $23,000. Interest starts to accrue on these loans six months after the student graduates, at which time repayments begin. Students who apply for aid are also eligible for *unsubsidized Stafford loans.* Interest on these loans begins to accrue immediately, although the borrower can defer the interest payment until he or she begins to repay the principal, typically after graduation. In most cases, students who accept a federally subsidized loan will be required to participate in the federal work-study program, in which students are given on-campus jobs and are expected to work between 10 and 15 hours a week.

State loans may also make up part of your aid package. Most states also have loan programs for students who live or go to school in that state.

LOANS FOR PARENTS

One of the most attractive and often overlooked options for parents is the federal Parent Loan for Undergraduate Students (PLUS Loan). Rates on PLUS loans may be cheaper than those for home equity loans, in some cases making it a wise idea to rethink the traditional route of taking out a second mortgage to pay for your kid's education. Parents can borrow money no matter how much money they make. PLUS loans allow parents to borrow up to the total cost of four years of college, minus any financial aid received. As of 2006, this loan is available to graduate students as well. O'Brien says this can really help parents who haven't been able to save enough money for college. "You can borrow up to 100% of the cost of attendance—and that includes pens, pencils, travel—the whole gamut of higher education expenses. There are no income restrictions—even Bill Gates could qualify."

You do need to have a good credit rating, but if you can get a mortgage, you can get this loan. The downside is that you have to start paying back these loans pretty quickly. Repayment begins 60 days after you receive the loan, although you can stretch repayment over 10 years. The interest rate is fixed at 8.5%.

The rule of thumb used to be: use your house to pay for college by taking out a home equity loan or line of credit. That's what my parents did for me and my sister. But that's not necessarily the wisest strategy anymore. Recently, rates on PLUS loans have been far better than most rates on home loans.

Also keep in mind, interest on Stafford, and PLUS, and consolidation loans is tax-deductible and the interest is simple, not compounding like a home loan. So you'll never have to pay interest accrued on prior interest. You can also write off up to $2,500 in student loan interest on your federal income taxes up to certain income levels. One other advantage: There is a death benefit on these college loans. If the borrower dies, the loan is forgiven.

SPECIAL CIRCUMSTANCES

Be sure to let the financial aid office know if your circumstances changed after the application was signed, sealed, and delivered. If you lose your job or your income drastically changes while your child is in college, or after you initially fill out the financial aid forms, the college can update your needs analysis. Just write a letter explaining what has happened to change your situation, enclosing supporting documents, such as a letter that shows what date your job was terminated. The college can issue what is known as a "professional judgment," which can lower your family's estimated contribution and make you eligible for federal, state, or institutional aid, or at least more loans.

SCHOLARSHIPS

Not happy with your aid offer? Unable to negotiate a better package? Try to score some scholarships. Ideally, your child should begin searching for possible sources for scholarships in his or her sophomore year of high school to find out what qualifications are necessary for the various programs. Jasmine, a 2004 graduate of the University of Central Arkansas, did just that—and financed her entire four years with free money. Jasmine, who is African American, received a few awards designated specifically for minority students, but the bulk of scholarship aid was based on her academic record or community service.

About 7% of college students win some type of scholarship to finance their education and the typical award is about $2,000. Many Web sites offer free scholarship searches. Just make sure your child fills out the questionnaires thoroughly. "You've got to have information about what your educational level is, what you plan to study, where you live, your ethnicity—all of those things go into our database and allow us to match scholarship programs with your unique requirements," says Baird Johnson of Fast-Web (*www.fastweb.monster.com*), one of the leading scholarship search Web sites. Other sites include *www.finaid.org* and *www.srnexpress.com*; the College Board also has a free scholarship search on its Web site, *www.collegeboard.com.*

You may find scholarships based on your family's ethnicity, place of worship, or association with certain clubs or community organizations—or even where you shop. Several department stores and discount retailers offer scholarships to high school students with above-average academic performance. Some of the most unusual scholarships can prove the most lucrative. Duck brand duct tape hosts a prom contest where the company awards two $2,500 scholarships to a couple whose prom outfits are made entirely of duct tape. There are also scholarships for tall students, short students, left-handed students, skateboarders, and even students who can call ducks (it's true!).

If you look hard enough, you'll probably find some scholarship program for your child. Finding a way to use other people's money to fund your child's education can help you focus on growing your own fund for your financial dreams.

6

HEALTHY, WEALTHY, AND WISE

Invest in Your Health by Choosing the Right Plans (Health, Disability, and Long-Term Care Insurance).

Robert and Kathy are health care freaks—they are both healthy, and yet they spend a lot of time thinking about their medical coverage. The pair, who own a small electrical equipment distributor business in Indiana, probably employ more hours calculating their health care expenses than the average couple. Under their health insurance plan, they are responsible for paying the full tab for all medical costs for themselves and their son up to their $5,000 deductible, including routine doctor's visits and prescriptions for themselves and their teenage son. The family has been healthy over the past few years, but Kathy says she does think twice about going to the doctor. "You don't run to the doctor for every little sniffle or cough or anything like that because you're coming home with a $90 doctor bill instead of a $10 copay."

On the other hand, Sally and Ron usually only focus on their health care needs once a year. Ron works for a major investment firm in Manhattan. Sally, a mortgage broker, works on commission. The family relies on the health insurance provided by Ron's employer, but Sally says she is the one who pores over the benefits materials during the company's open enrollment period to figure out which insurance plan will be the most comprehensive and most economical for their family. She finds the process overwhelming.

When it comes to making health care decisions, most couples are more like Sally and Ron. They have no idea what their health care actually costs. Nearly two-thirds of women are responsible for family health care decisions, but according to a survey by Aetna and the Financial Planning Association, 35% do not know basic information about health benefits, and more than half have trouble choosing a health plan. Health care coverage is like good health itself—most people only worry about it after it's gone. People don't think about the *real* cost of health care until they switch jobs and compare the benefits packages of various employers, or until they lose their job—and their health care coverage—and are forced to foot their own medical bills. Deciding among traditional insurance, the alphabet soup of managed care plans (HMO, POS, and PPO), or one of the directed health plans presents a challenge to many couples. If you work for different companies, you need to compare health care providers and plans provided by each employer. You must figure out whether children should be covered under one or both plans. If you are self-employed or run your own business and are responsible for choosing your own insurance coverage, you need to know where to go to find the best, and most affordable, health care plan.

For couples, investing in your health also means planning for unforeseen emergencies as well as situations where one or both of you may become disabled and unable to work full-time or even part-time. You need to build a nest egg of income to take care of yourself, your spouse, and your family. That is why it is so important to have disability insurance. You also need to plan for the day when you and your spouse may be unable to take care of each other. Your children may not be able to help you financially and you may need to pay for nursing home care or some form of assisted living. Long-term care insurance is another critical component of health care planning. So how do you know if you have the right kind of insurance for you and your family? Read on for more information on different types of plans, and how to choose the right one, to make sure your health care is covered.

Employers are increasingly calling on their employees to pick up a larger part of the tab, so figuring out these costs—what your health benefits are actually worth—is critical, and even more so when you have a job with little or no health care benefits. In 2006, Fidelity Investments announced that a couple without employer-sponsored health care during retirement needed to set aside $200,000 to pay for health care costs after the age of 65. That's four times more than most people make in a year. And the number has been rising at an average of 5.8% every year. The shock of that stat is enough to make you want to go out on disability.

So you need to take stock. There are ways to evaluate the benefits you are getting. Your first stop should be a visit to your employer's human resources department.

Here are the five questions to ask:

1. How much are your health benefits worth?
2. What percentage of those benefits must you pay for?
3. What is your contribution?
4. What is the employer's contribution?
5. What types of health plans are available to you?

The answer to the last question will result in a lot more homework for you. You and your spouse will need to consider the services you use the most and then compare various plans to help you get the biggest bang for your health care bucks.

THE ALPHABET SOUP OF HEALTH CARE

As employers offer more choices in health insurance plans to their workers, deciding which plan makes sense is becoming more difficult because there are so many factors to consider. Luckily, the basics of what you need to know about each type of plan are all right here—the pros and cons, as well as suggestions on the compromises you and your spouse may need to make so that an employer's cookie-cutter health plan will fit your medical and financial needs.

UNDERSTANDING HEALTH CARE COSTS

When Christina's allergist suggested that she should begin getting allergy shots regularly, the 36-year-old wasn't worried about needles; she was concerned about costs. "Shots are a long-term-investment, and an expensive long-term investment," she said. She also was cognizant of the fact that she was moving from employer health coverage to an individual policy that she had to purchase herself. She was fearful that her premiums might be bumped up if she was seen as an expensive patient. Christina ended up getting a second opinion from another allergist who shared her view that the shots weren't needed.

It's a good idea to listen to one's doctor. It's also a good idea to have an understanding of the health care system and where one's treatment fits in. Overall, health care costs have seen double-digit increases for most of the decade. Fortunately, the typical employee covered by health insurance at work pays only about 27% of premiums for family coverage, with their employers paying the rest.* Yet you still may notice your out-of-pocket medical costs are mounting. Some prescription drugs and treatments may not be covered by your insurance. Or you may receive only partial payment for a visit to a doctor or dentist because he or she is not on your insurer's preferred list of providers. Most workers now have to pay some sort of deductible before their health coverage even kicks in. So that is why it is becoming increasingly important for you to know what you're paying for.

Rising health care costs are inevitable. If you are not prepared for them when they hit, health care expenses can wipe out your savings—including

---

*2006 *Employer Health Benefits* Survey by the Kaiser Family Foundation and the Health Research and Educational Trust (HRET).

money you've put away for a home, college tuition, or a vacation. Premiums for employer-sponsored health coverage rose nearly 8% on average in 2006. Family health coverage now costs an average of $11,480 a year, with workers paying an average of $2,973 toward those premiums, about $1,354 more than in 2000.

Instead of raising premiums for all workers, employers are trying to shift costs to patients who use the most medical services. So copayments for visits to specialists will rise. In addition to deductibles for overall coverage, you may also be responsible for deductibles based on services, such as hospital admission or a trip to the emergency room, as well as separate deductibles for prescription medications. Many plans are also switching from copayments to coinsurance for prescription drugs. That means that instead of paying a flat dollar amount per prescription, you'll pay a percentage of the actual cost.

There are a couple of great Web sites that can help you sort all this out. Log on to *www.planforyourhealth.com*. Aetna, one of the nation's leading health insurers, and the Financial Planning Association teamed up to create tools, like "Your Health Benefit Priorities," to help you evaluate your health benefits package by gauging what you really need from your health benefits plan and the aspects of a plan that are most important to you. (Also, see the "Health Needs Worksheet" and "Choosing the Right Health Plan Questionnaire" at the end of this book.)

If you value your existing relationship with your physician, are concerned about your spouse's and children's health care expenses, and want to keep your copayments relatively low, the site suggests you consider contributing to a flexible spending account (FSA).

On the other hand, if you have a chronic illness, would prefer to see specialists without a referral, and want to keep your prescription costs down, you should find out if your employer offers coverage for prescription drugs, dental, or long-term health care. Also, depending on your pharmacy benefits, generic and over-the-counter medications may decrease your pharmacy costs. So you should check with your doctor to see if any of those drugs may be right for you.

OPEN ENROLLMENT PERIOD

Halloween may be a hallmark of the fall season, but health care options offered by your employer designated as "open enrollment" also happen that time of year, and it can be really scary. New plans may be added as options and old plans are taken away. Just as your health situation changes—you decide to have a baby, your child develops asthma, your husband is diagnosed with diabetes—the type of coverage you choose may need to change as well.

Use the open enrollment period to make a budget for your health care needs. Think about the medical costs you incurred this year and whether they will be the same, higher, or lower next year. Figure out what suits your cash flow needs: higher premium and lower out-of-pocket costs or vice versa. Determine how much money you will spend on medical expenses and stash that cash in a flexible spending account. Finally, you can calculate the effect these health care deductions will have on your take-home pay by using a handy Web site: *www.paycheckcity.com.*

CALCULATE THE COSTS

You don't want to just pick the plan that offers the greatest number of benefits or the plan that will take the smallest bite out of your wallet. You need to focus on the total cost—deductibles, copayments, and premiums. Figuring out how each plan fits into your budget may take a few calculations. You'll need to add up the amount you'll pay each month as a premium as well as what you're likely to shell out over the coming year for doctors' visits, prescription drugs, and medical services. Take advantage of company-provided calculators. Some will allow workers to model the costs of different plans based on the health claims they filled the previous year. Go to the "Health Expense Calculator" on the *PlanForYourHealth.com* site to help you estimate your annual medical, dental, vision, and prescription expenses based upon your age, conditions, and frequency of doctor's office visits. Calculating what you spend today may help you determine where you can cut back to reduce health care costs in the future.

If you can't do the calculations online, gather your old receipts and consider the services you need most or have used most in the past. Then compare the plans by looking at each part of the plan—premium, deductible, copayments, limits—and asking the following questions:

- PREMIUM (The amount charged, often in installments, for an insurance policy): How much is the monthly premium?
- DEDUCTIBLE (A fixed amount that an individual must pay for covered medical services before the health plan will pay benefits): If there is a deductible, how much will I have to pay before the plan starts to pay for care? What is the deductible for in-network care? What is the deductible for using out-of-network providers? Is there a separate hospital deductible?
- COPAYMENT (A specified dollar amount or percentage a patient is required to contribute toward the cost of covered medical services under a health plan): How much do I have to pay each time I use a service? What is the copayment for a doctor who is in the network? Out of network?
- SPECIAL COPAYMENT: How much is a regular doctor's visit? Emergency-room visit? Mental health treatment? What is the copayment on brand-name drugs? Generic drugs? Specialty services, such as radiation?
- ANNUAL LIMITS: How many days in the hospital will the plan cover? What is the limit on spending per beneficiary? Is there a limit on the number of visits or services (especially for mental health or physical therapy)?
- MAXIMUM OUT-OF-POCKET/LIFETIME LIMIT: Some health benefit plans limit the total amount of benefits an individual

may receive or limit the number of particular services an individual may receive over the term of the policy. Find out if there is a maximum amount of out-of-pocket costs that you may incur and, on the flip side, what is the lifetime limit of coverage that you will receive with each plan. How much total coverage can you expect with the plan?

Getting answers to these questions will help you figure out your response to the one that is most important: What type of coverage is right for me and my spouse or me and my family? Since it will no doubt be costing you more each year, you want to make sure you're shelling out those extra bucks for the plan that best serves your needs, your spouse's needs, and your family's needs.

TRADITIONAL FEE-FOR-SERVICE PLANS

Pros. If you value flexibility and don't mind paying higher premiums and out-of-pocket expenses, then you may want to consider a fee-for-service plan. You choose your doctors and hospitals. You can visit any specialist you want and you don't have to go to your regular doctor for an appointment that essentially consists of him simply writing a referral to allow you to see the specialist you wanted to see in the first place. Another plus: the health care provider you choose is not subject to the approval of your insurer, although the service must be covered by the plan. The doctor you choose may charge more for some services than the insurance company pays. You'll have to make up the difference.

Cons. Be careful because costs can add up quickly. There is typically a deductible before the insurance company starts paying the claims. Then you are responsible for copayments of about 20% of "reasonable and customary" medical expenses. A "reasonable expense" is a limit set by a health plan on the amount it will pay for a medical service. This limit is often determined by referring to amounts typically charged for a particular health care service by other providers in the same geographic area. With a traditional fee-for-service plan, doctors are reimbursed for about 80% of the bill, but you might have to pay medical costs upfront and then apply for reimbursement from the insurance company. That can mean cash that's out of your hands for months. Also, the insurer does not always agree to pay its 80%. If the medical services are not deemed "reasonable," you may never see that money.

Tip: You may be able to lower your premiums by choosing a higher deductible (at least $1,000 to $2000 for an individual and $2,000 to $5,000 for a family) and invest what you save in premiums in a tax-deductible health savings account that you can tap into to pay out-of-pocket expenses. Money that you don't use in a given year grows tax-free to pay for future medical costs.

HEALTH MAINTENANCE ORGANIZATION (HMO)

Pros. Many young families find getting HMO coverage is the most cost-effective option. If you want a plan that is the least expensive, you'll probably opt for an HMO. Pay a monthly premium and all of your medical care and services through the HMO are covered. You can have exorbitant medical bills and as long as your health care providers are within the HMO network, you'll only have to pay $15 to $25 per doctor's visit or for having prescriptions filled. So your cash flow can stay constant and you don't have to worry about filling out loads of paperwork to get reimbursed for services. Newlyweds or young families who don't want to scout for doctors may prefer one-stop shopping. And if you are on a tight budget, you'll have a better idea of your monthly medical costs. If you use doctors and hospitals within the HMO network, routine and preventative care will be covered, as well as medical catastrophes.

Cons. Keep in mind, HMOs are also the least flexible of all insurance plans. You must choose a primary care physician, or PCP. You may be required to get a referral from your PCP to see a specialist. And, you can only go to the HMO's participating doctors and hospitals or the insurer won't pay the full tab.

(POINT-OF-SERVICE) POS

Your HMO may also have a POS (point of service) option. POS plans are more flexible than HMOs, but they usually still require you to select a primary care physician.

Pros. You may be able to visit a doctor outside the network and still receive coverage—although the amount covered will be substantially less than if you had gone to a physician within the network.

Cons. To go out-of-network, you may need permission from your PCP first. The cost for visiting an out-of-network doctor is tied to a percentage of the usual and customary fee schedule. If you want even greater flexibility, the next option may be best for you.

PREFERRED PROVIDER ORGANIZATION (PPO)

Pros. PPOs are kind of a compromise between traditional fee-for-service plans and HMOs. You have control over your choice of doctors (including specialists), hospitals, and pharmacies within a network of providers established by the insurance company. You don't need permission from your primary care physician to see specialists who are in the network.

Cons. Costs can add up if you go outside the network. If the provider is within the network, you generally make a small copayment, say $15 for a routine office visit. But if you go outside the network, you may have to pay the entire bill yourself and then submit it for reimbursement. Usually there is a deductible and only 80% of the "reasonable and customary" costs are covered (you pay the other 20%) or you pay the difference between what network doctors and out-of-network doctors charge.

CONSUMER-DIRECTED HEALTH PLANS

Employers are increasingly requiring employees to select consumer-directed health plans to give workers more control over their health care spending. In these plans, the employer provides much of what is offered in a traditional plan, but also includes an account that you manage yourself. A consumer-directed plan may include a flexible spending account (FSA), health savings account (HSA), and/or a health reimbursement arrangement (HRA).

FLEXIBLE SPENDING ACCOUNT (FSA)

Flexible spending accounts are part of the tax law that enables employers to let workers set aside pretax dollars to pay medical costs that are not covered by insurance. Eligible expenses include over-the-counter medications, dentures, contact lenses, eyeglasses, as well as insurance premiums and prescriptions. Dietary supplements and products used for general health maintenance are not reimbursable. Check to see what's allowed at *www.irs. gov.* Look for publication 502.

The big downside to these accounts is that you must "use it or lose it." Unused money becomes the property of your employer at the end of the year. Some plans extend the date to March 15 of the next year. Check with your plan. While it is a great benefit, be careful how much money you allocate to these accounts to make sure you use every penny wisely. See if there's a flexible spending calculator on your plan's Web site, or use the one on the Kiplinger Web site, *www.kiplinger.com/tools/flex,* to figure out how much money you should put into an FSA account. Keep in mind, you'll lose the unused money in an FSA account if you leave the company.

HEALTH SAVINGS ACCOUNT (HSA)

Rick, a newly married, 32-year-old printing company manager, decided to take more control of his health care by switching to a new health insurance plan that has lower monthly premiums. He also started putting a portion of his pay into a tax-free health savings account, or HSA. The money comes directly out of his paycheck and goes to this special account. The HSA is another way to save for out-of-pocket medical expenses, including prescription and over-the-counter drugs, and you don't have to spend every penny each year (as you do with a flexible spending account, or FSA). If you budget appropriately for what you will spend, you can also build up health care savings for years to come.

In 2006, individuals could contribute up to $2,700 to the account and $5,150 for families. The money can be used for medical expenses this year, next, or down the road. This was a big incentive for Rick. "I will have money toward my retirement that I can use toward my premiums, those types of things, once I retire," he says.

Contributions, much like a traditional individual retirement account, are tax-free and grow tax-free. HSA withdrawals are also tax-free and there are no income limitations. And unlike flexible spending accounts, unused money in the account can be rolled over from year to year, accumulating more tax-free savings. So if you leave or lose your job, the money in the account is still yours to use for future health care expenses.

HSAs offer a tax-free way to save for current and future health care needs. As long as you have a high-deductible insurance policy, you can stash cash in an HSA. Anyone is eligible as long as they are under 65 years of age and are already covered by a health insurance policy with an annual deductible of at least $1,000 if you're single, and $2,000 for families. Log on to *www.hsainsider.com* to find insurance companies in your state that offer these accounts.

HEALTH REIMBURSEMENT ARRANGEMENT (HRA)

Your employer funds the HRA and you use the money to pay deductibles and covered medical expenses. You don't count the funds as income, but you can't draw them out in cash either. And if you leave the company, you lose the HRA.

Pros. A consumer-directed plan with an HRA may be for you if you're healthy or if the medical care you require isn't covered by your current insurer and you can afford to pay the deductible before traditional plan benefits begin. Unused money in your HRA usually rolls over to the next year.

Cons. Switching to a consumer-directed plan requires that you pay attention to the *real* costs of regular doctor's office visits and specialist services. Check with your current insurance plan to find out the real expense. The insurer should have records of the services you use and should be able to tell you exactly what they cost.

THE COBRA BRIDGE

HMO, POS, PPO, traditional insurance, and consumer-driven health plans can be great options for the right couple or family. But what happens when a working spouse loses his or her job? Well, you and your family don't necessarily have to lose your health benefits—at least not right away.

If you are unemployed (or worry that you'll lose your job), the law guarantees that you can maintain your health insurance coverage. Under COBRA (the Consolidated Omnibus Budget Reconciliation Act) employers with group health plans must offer you insurance for up to 18

PRESCRIPTION DRUG COVERAGE

The typical family spends most of its medical money on prescription drugs. If you and your spouse each have prescription drug coverage, investigate how these plans work. Many companies now offer "three-tier" coverage, with the lowest copayment for generic drugs, a higher one for the drugs on the plan's "formulary" (approved list of drugs), and the highest copayment for nonformulary, brand-name medications. The formularies are usually on the health plans' Web sites, so make sure that any drugs that you use regularly are included there. If your regular prescription is second-tier on one plan and third-tier on another, it can mean the difference of $20 to $30 every time you get it filled. When you visit your doctor, take along your health plan's list of approved drugs and ask your doctor if he or she could prescribe a generic or less costly version of the medication. There may also be a "mail-order" discount. Health benefit plans often offer distribution of prescribed medication directly to the patient through the mail. Since mail-order distributors can purchase drugs in larger volumes than can retail outlets, the cost charged to patients is often lower. See if the "maintenance" drugs that you or your family take regularly can be ordered through the mail.

Insurance companies are also starting to place hospitals in tiers based on how expensive they are or on the firm's measure of quality. If your hospital of choice is given a less favorable ranking, you may face reduced coverage if you use the facility. For instance, your deductible may be $500 instead of $200. So find out which hospital your doctor sends patients to and how it ranks. If you want or think you will need an expensive, cutting-edge hospital when you're sick, decide whether you'd rather pay for that with higher premiums now or absorb the extra costs if you should ever need care.

months after you leave your job for any reason other than gross incompetence.

You'll get seamless coverage and it will probably be less expensive than what you can get in the open market. Try to get it as soon as you are out of

PREGNANCY AND HEALTH INSURANCE

If you change health plans while you're pregnant, your new insurer can't deny claims related to your pregnancy. Federal law bars pregnancy from being considered a preexisting condition. But pregnant women can still get caught with no insurance coverage for their prenatal care if they don't plan carefully. Under a law known as HIPAA, the Health Insurance Portability and Accountability Act of 1996, health insurers cannot deny you coverage when you go from one job to another and switch health plans.

Unfortunately, there are some loopholes. HIPAA doesn't apply to someone who previously had no health coverage at all and then gets into a group health plan through a new job. If you and your spouse are thinking about having a baby, make sure you check out your policy to find out what coverage you have.

---

work. Don't wait. You only have 60 days after leaving your job to sign up for COBRA, or you'll be ineligible for benefits. Visit *www.cobrainsurance.net* to find out more about this program.

Tip: COBRA will generally be more expensive than the premiums you paid to your employer's health plan while you were working.

INDIVIDUAL COVERAGE

One out of seven Americans has no health insurance at all. But you can bet that seven out of seven Americans get sick at some point in their lives. When you haven't invested in your health, an accident or illness can be disastrous. Medical bills are among the biggest contributors to personal bankruptcies. Sure, health insurance is expensive, but that doesn't mean you should forgo it. A smarter choice may be to opt for high-deductible policies. That will help keep your monthly premiums down. You'll be responsible for more out-of-pocket costs (since the deductible could be $1,000 to $5,000), but that will help you keep better track of your medical expenses and overall monthly cash flow.

If you own a business, are self-employed, or have joined the ranks of the unemployed who have exhausted their COBRA benefits and are not covered on your spouse's plan, you probably now have to start looking at individual health insurance plans. One way around that, used by about one-third of self-employed workers, is to have an employed spouse who gets a family policy at work. If you lose your job (or are fired), your spouse has 30 days to put the whole family on his or her workplace policy, even if the employer normally restricts signing up for an insurance plan in the middle of the year.

Coverage and premiums on these policies can vary widely, so start by contacting five or six insurance agents who specialize in individual polices for quotes and information about the type of coverage in your area. You may find that you cannot afford the same level of coverage that was offered by your previous employer. You might find the most cost-effective plan is one that provides only a few primary-care benefits, even though it means shelling out cash for services that employer's plans regularly subsidize.

If you live in or near a large metropolitan area, chances are you'll be able to choose from many large and small insurance firms offering a wide menu of benefit plans. Compare quotes from licensed insurers on the Web by logging on to *www.ehealthinsurance.com* or *www.insure.com*. Tap into professional connections. Unions and associations may have discount rates on health insurance.

Make sure you check out the insurer. By law, those who underwrite or sell insurance must be licensed by the state, but few customers bother to find out if the insurance carrier is licensed. Check with your state insurance or health department. For links to all state insurance commission Web sites, go to *www.naic.org*. Also check the company's financial soundness with a rating firm like A.M. Best (*www.ambest.com*).

HEALTH INSURANCE FOR THE SELF-EMPLOYED

Although getting individual or family coverage on your own is expensive, if you're self-employed, the good news is you could get a nice tax break on your medical expenses to offset some of these costs. First of all, you should set up a tax-deductible health savings account (discussed earlier in this chapter). You can also deduct from your self-employment earnings 100% of the health insurance premiums you pay, up from 70% in 2002 and 30% in 1996. Unfortunately, if you are eligible for any employer-sponsored health plan, including your spouse's, you aren't supposed to claim this deduction, even if you aren't on your spouse's plan.

Some applicants for individual health insurance are rejected outright and others can't qualify for standard-price policies because of preexisting medical conditions that put them at higher risk for having high health care costs. Don't give up. If you've been turned down for insurance, about 30 states have a high-risk pool for health coverage. And there are other alternatives: check out *www.healthinsuranceinfo.net,* run by Georgetown University's Institute for Health Care Research and Policy. It offers consumer guides to health care options for each state.

CHOOSING THE RIGHT HEALTH PLAN

For our parents' generation, getting a good job meant employment with a benefits package—and those benefits included a traditional medical insurance plan, period. If there was any choice, it was between that conventional plan and a precursor to what is known today as a health maintenance organization (HMO). Today, we not only have to figure out the best benefits for ourselves, we also have to decide how to integrate them with those offered by our spouse's or partner's employer.

If both spouses are working, the couple's initial instinct may be to keep separate plans, but health benefits could be less expensive for a couple under one plan. You may both be able to be covered under both plans, but you need to check with your employers to make sure. Chris and I tried that for a few years, but when I was pregnant with our second child I found it was not such a bargain. My ob/gyn was an "in-network" provider under my husband's plan, but not mine. Yet since I had insurance through my employer, I had to submit all claims through that insurer and have them denied before resubmitting them to my husband's insurance company. Sound confusing? It was, though in the end my prenatal, labor, delivery, and postnatal visits were all covered.

Many companies coordinate benefits to make sure each of you pays something. So the decision becomes whether each spouse should go with their employer's insurance individually, or go together on one plan. And, if you go together, whose plan should you choose? Since our primary care physician and our son's and daughter's pediatrician are in *my* insurer's provider network, Chris and I decided to put the whole family on my insurance coverage.

Childless couples may find that "splitting up" the insurance, opting for premiums for "self-only" coverage for each spouse, is cheaper than "family" coverage. Some companies also offer a credit to workers who decline health insurance, and if either of you has that option, it should be factored into your calculations.

Be sure to double check the policy terms on your employer's health plan every year because they often will change.

Finding the plan with the lowest premium and fewest out-of-pocket expenses isn't always the best strategy. To compare two or more plans, answer the "Choosing the Right Health Plan Questionnaire" at the end of the book. You may not be able to give simple "yes" or "no" answers to the questions. But the details that you include should help you think about and compare your health plan choices.

Choice of doctors is usually the biggest selling point with an insurance plan. So before you enroll, ask to see the plan's roster of physicians. Make sure there are plenty of choices in the specialties you may need. Also, call the doctors you want to use to make sure they are still providers for that plan and are accepting new patients.

Plans offered by your employer may be rated in *Consumer Reports* or you may be able to find a "report card" on them at the National Committee for Quality Assurance's Web site at *www.ncqa.org.* The NCQA reviews appeals and health plan denial records, interviews staff, and conducts audits on consumer surveys. It rates plans on, among other things, access to doctors, chronic-care treatment, the number of qualified providers, and customer service. You can also call your state insurance department to see whether the plan has received consumer complaints.

Remember to follow up. Report any problems with the plan to your company's benefits department immediately.

DENTAL AND VISION COVERAGE

If you work for a large company, you probably have a dental plan. Yet, there are differences among the dental insurance and dental "discount" plans offered by most major companies. With dental insurance, you pay regular premiums for your coverage and your plan has spending caps. It generally covers 100% of the cost of preventive services after you meet your deductible. (However, many dental programs have limits on orthodontia and some do not cover orthodontia for adults at all.) Dental discount plans are not insurance— these are membership-based programs. Members pay a fee and, in exchange, they get discounts on a variety of dental services, such as fillings, braces, exams, and routine cleanings. Members typically receive about 30% off standard out-of-pocket prices. With a dental discount plan, you must go to a dentist who has agreed to participate in the plan and offer services at a discounted price. The wave of consumer-driven health care has hit the dental benefits market as well. Direct reimbursement dental plans give you the free-dom to choose any dentist. You pay the full amount of services directly to your dentist, get a receipt, and show it to your employer. You are reimbursed for all or part of the dental costs from a special benefits fund established by your employer.

Dental insurance often comes with an annual payout limit, so pricey den-tal treatments probably won't be fully covered. Find out how much of the dental and vision premiums your company picks up. Often there is little or no subsidy with vision plans, so signing up for this policy is no bargain.

Compare how much you would likely spend for everything out of pocket versus what the premiums, deductibles, copayments, and uncovered treat-ments together would cost you. One strategy may be to sign up for coverage every other year and time checkups at the beginning and end of the year. But knowing you must pay a set premium every month may help you keep to a household budget. Also, dentists and ophthalmologists often charge unin-sured patients more.

DISABILITY INSURANCE

Josie, an obstetrician, who is healthy today, knows an accident or illness could jeopardize her livelihood and her family's financial well-being tomor-row. She held the same disability policy for the first eight years of her prac-tice, and then decided it was time to increase her coverage to the maximum she could get. "If something happened to me and I'm not able to do an ultra-sound or examine a patient, I'm unemployed," she says. Her new disability income policy pays her about 60% of her gross income up to age 65, a typi-cal payout for most individual policies.

You probably think your biggest asset is your house or your 401(k), but it is really your ability to earn money. What would happen to your cash flow if you were injured or became ill and could not work? Social Security provides disability benefits, if you qualify, but those funds probably won't be enough for you and your family to maintain even the most basic standard of living. The Social Security Administration says the average monthly payment to a disabled worker in 2006 was $944.50. For a disabled worker with a spouse and two or more children, the average payment was about $1,753. Your state worker's compensation fund usually provides benefits only if you get hurt on the job. The payments typically last only a few years and are pretty low. Like Social Security disability benefits, it may help pay a few small bills, but don't count on it to cover your living expenses.

No policy will replace 100% of your income. So if you do become disabled, you may have to change your lifestyle if not your entire life. Even with her expanded coverage, says Josie, if something happened to her, "I'd have to live on a better budget than I'm doing right now."

Your employer may provide some kind of short-term disability coverage, but the checks will end after three months to a year. Your emergency reserves may last a few months, but then what? If you're working and need income to live, you need disability insurance. The only time you don't need it is if you are so rich that you could live comfortably for the rest of your life and be able to pay for your children's college education, a new home, and retirement without any extra money.

"There are only three things that can happen to all of us. We live a very long and healthy life. We die prematurely. We succumb to a disability (through an accident or illness)," says New Jersey financial adviser Altair Gobo. "The question is: Does your financial plan work under each scenario? If there is a financial shortfall due to death or disability, then insurance should be a consideration."

When it comes to trying to figure out how much disability insurance you should get, try to get as much as you can—as much as the insurer will issue you, because they most likely will not cover your full salary. Take a look at your household budget and your emergency reserves and determine how long you will be able to cover your expenses. Then you can determine how much of your income you will have to supplement.

There are four main variables to figuring how much it will cost you:

- *monthly benefit:* Most disability policies have a fixed monthly benefit that does not increase with time, although you can purchase extra coverage or riders that offer higher payment schedules.
- *definition of disability:* Become familiar with these terms: "own occ," which means you are unable to perform the duties of your specific occupation, and "any occ," the inability to perform the duties of any job for which your education and training make you qualified.
- *waiting period:* This is the amount of time you must be disabled before the benefit kicks in. It can range from one week to two years. The longer you wait the less your disability policy will cost.
- *benefit period:* That is how long you will receive monthly benefits once your policy starts paying, and this period can range from six months to life.

You may also want to consider certain riders that could add to the cost, such as a rider that pays only if you can remain at work or return to work part-time, or an additional purchase option that guarantees you the right to buy additional disability insurance in the future regardless of your health at the time.

If you are disabled and can't work, long-term disability insurance steps in to give you a portion of your pay. Many employers offer long-term disability policies in their benefits package. Either the company pays for it or the worker can buy it at discounted group rates. Generally workers can buy coverage that typically replaces up to 60% of their pay. Some companies let you pay for the policy with pretax dollars (although the benefits will be taxable); others use after-tax money (in this case, benefits are not taxed). It can be a toss-up as to the best way to pay since pretax is better if you don't become disabled and after-tax is preferable if you do. Some employers provide disability coverage for free but many companies are putting limits on the coverage, cutting benefits after two years. Purchased through your employer, coverage is often paid until you turn 65. But if you buy coverage yourself, you own the policy and benefits will continue as long as you qualify for them.

Group plans also may not provide a sufficient benefit. But if you also have an individual policy, the two combined often add up to adequate coverage. You may be able to purchase supplemental coverage by paying extra for more group coverage through your employer or by getting an individual policy. You may be able to get 50 or 60% of the coverage provided by your employer and then increase that to 70 or 75% by buying supplemental coverage through your employer.

Group plans are generally less expensive, but the problem is that if you leave or lose your job, you'll often lose your coverage. Average premiums on individual policies cost about 2 to 3% of your gross income. But remember, those policies are also portable. You own it and you'll always have coverage even if you switch jobs. Many individual policies will even cover retirement contributions as part of your gross income.

Disability insurance is not cheap and costs will vary based on your age, your health, the length of time you can wait before the benefit kicks in, and the duration of the benefit. But there are ways to cut costs and lower premiums:

- Buy it early.
- Choose a policy with the broadest definition of disability (policies that say you are insured for a disability in your own occupation are more expensive than those that consider you disabled if you cannot perform any occupation).
- Cut back on the amount of income that is protected.
- Increase the elimination or waiting period before starting the payout (extending it to 90 or 180 days would be cheaper than 60 days).
- Shorten the benefit period (make it only 5 or 10 years rather than extending to age 65).

The best trade-off may be to keep a longer benefit period and extend the waiting period, as long as you have adequate emergency funds to cover expenses until the disability income kicks in.

As with health insurance, make sure you ask appropriate questions before buying the policy. For example, how does the policy treat pregnancy? Will it pay for partial disability? Is the gatekeeper your doctor or an insurance-company doctor? Also, ask about "stepped" premiums, which can allow the purchaser to pay about 35% less in the first five years.

LONG-TERM CARE INSURANCE

More than 12 million Americans are in a nursing home, assisted living center, or receive care at home. Almost 5 million of them are under the age of 65, yet most have no insurance against one of the most expensive realities of life: long-term care. As discussed earlier, don't expect the government to come in and cover the cost of health care in your Golden Years. Medicare covers only a few days of skilled nursing care after a hospital stay, and almost all assets and income must be spent down before state Medicaid will pick up the tab. And the tab is expensive. The national average daily rate at a nursing home runs $203 a day.* At two and a half years for the average stay, the cost climbs to over $185,000. Some researchers have predicted those costs will quadruple by the year 2030. That is why long-term care is so important.

It doesn't take a lot of extra planning. Many companies now offer long-term care insurance to their employees. A few years ago, the federal government launched the largest employer-sponsored long-term care program ever, offering this optional benefit to 20 million federal workers, retirees, and their spouses, parents, and adult children. If your employer does not

---

*Prudential survey of 2006 Private Nursing Home Room Costs.

offer this insurance, you can purchase a group long-term care policy through an organization like AARP or an individual plan for yourself and your spouse.

It's best to buy long-term care insurance when you're in good health, some insurance experts say maybe even as early as your 30s and 40s, and definitely by the time you're 50. If you're in your 30s or 40s, these policies are a bargain—at least compared with what they cost when you're old enough to need them. Use the checklist at *www.MetLife.com* to compare long-term care policies. Someone in their mid-30s, for example, could buy a plan for about $300 a year. Someone age 50 could buy a plan for $500 to $600. But if you wait until you're 70 years old, you may be facing a cost of about $2,000 a year. If you buy a long-term care policy from your employer, the coverage is usually available at a discount (up to 10%), with premiums deducted from your paycheck. But the savings you receive now may not be worth it, if you're likely to pay for the policy for many more years before you actually need it. Any insurance policy is a gamble. Here, you're making a bet that might not pay off for 40 years. Although experts' recommendations vary, buying a long-term care policy somewhere between age 50 and 60 definitely seems like a wise idea. Among the factors to consider:

• **Asset protection.** Long-term care insurance makes the most sense for people who have a net worth of somewhere between $100,000 and $2 million and are seeking to preserve their nest egg, says Robert Davis of Long-Term Care Quote. With the average cost of a nursing home running over $70,000 a year, $100,000 won't last very long. But if you have over $2 million at that time, you will probably be able to cover your own nursing home, assisted living, or home health care expenses. (Although some people buy the policies anyway to ensure that their health care costs don't eat up their children's potential inheritance.)

• **Family health history.** A chronic illness or medical condition that runs in your family and heightens your insurance risk could be a reason to buy the insurance now, since many employer-sponsored plans don't require health screenings.

- **Family support.** Do you live near family or friends who could step in as caregivers? If not, you should probably be planning for your long-term care.

If you decide to buy a long-term care policy now, make sure it has an alternate plan of care provision so that even if a service isn't explicitly covered in a plan today, if something new develops 10 years down the road, that alternate plan of care will be covered. Also think about how long a waiting or elimination period you can afford. This works like a deductible; the longer or higher it is, the lower the premium. And choose a policy with a benefit that at least matches the average daily nursing home rate in your area. Also make sure it has inflation protection, guaranteeing benefits will go up at least 5% a year.

In the end, the decision often comes down to dollars. The younger you are, the less expensive the premiums. And sometimes you can get better deals on the open market than you can at work. As with any type of insurance, it's important to compare rates and carriers. You can do that online at Long-Term Care Quote's Web site, *www.longtermcarequote.com, www.insure.com,* or through an insurance agent. Ask your state's department of insurance for their buyer's guide to long-term care insurance. Use the map at *http://www.naic.org* to find your state's insurance department. The National Association of Insurance Commissioners also publishes a "Shoppers Guide to Long-Term Care Insurance" available online at *http://www.naic.org.*

Make sure you've purchased a policy from a company that has a strong financial base and a history of providing this kind of insurance. Remember, this is a plan you may not need for 10 to 20 years or more down the road, so you want to make sure that the company you buy it from will be around.

HEALTH CARE IN RETIREMENT

If you've checked out retirement planning calculators on the Internet, you know that most of them assume that you'll only need about 70 to 80% of your preretirement income when you retire. After all, you won't have to spend money on 401(k) contributions, commuting, suits and dry cleaning, when you're spending half of the year golfing in Florida. But many of those calculations omit an important factor: the rising cost of health care. Medicare won't be able to pick up the whole tab. More and more companies are cutting back on retiree health benefits—don't expect your employer to cover your health care expenses either.

So play it smart. Assume you'll need 100% of your preretirement income to get you through your Golden Years. If you can save that much, and you're healthy, and end up using less than that amount, that's great—that just means more vacations and trips to see the grandkids. But plan on needing all of your current income for now.

7

GET A LIFE (JACKET)

Insure Your Life and Property to Protect
Your Family and Finances.

Coaches in almost any team sport tend to preach the same thing—a good defense is a good offense. Defense wins games. You should use this motto when it comes to your finances too; it's good to be proactive. It also pays to play "D." You've got to work hard to preserve what you've made. One way of doing that is by taking out plenty of insurance.

Insurance is always a gamble. You pay now to protect yourself against something that may never happen or won't happen for years down the road. Yet having adequate insurance to cover catastrophic losses that you and your spouse would have difficulty covering on your own is an essential component of a financial plan. The five "must-haves" in insurance include (1) a comprehensive health policy or managed care plan (see chapter 6); (2) disability insurance to cover your loss of income when you can't work—especially for the primary breadwinner (also see Chapter 6); (3) a life insurance policy that will make up for your contribution to the family's expenses if you should die; and (4) homeowners and (5) auto insurance to repair or replace lost property and to protect you against liability claims. Failing to insure your income, it should be noted, is like forgetting to buy home insurance, only worse. Without that paycheck, you won't be able to afford the house. Making sure your insurance coverage fits your needs should be an annual resolution. When you change jobs or have a child, buy a new house or remodel your current home, or get a new car, it's important to look out for gaps in coverage to make sure your out-of-pocket expenses are as low as possible. Having adequate insurance is the best way to protect your financial plan.

LIFE INSURANCE

WHO NEEDS IT?

If your death would leave your spouse or children in a financial bind, then you definitely need life insurance. If you work, your salary may be essential to helping pay the mortgage, buy groceries, and save for your kids' education. For a stay-at-home parent, consider that your spouse would most likely have to pay someone to provide child care. Either way, you need to take out a life insurance policy. For parents, the life insurance coverage should last at least until your youngest child gets through college. Even if you don't have children, you may need life insurance to cover expenses that you share with your spouse. But if your spouse can live on his or her income and you don't have a mortgage, you may need only enough insurance to cover funeral expenses. Also, if you have accumulated a huge nest egg that could be subject to estate taxes, get insured so that your heirs can use the tax-free proceeds of the life insurance policy to pay off those liabilities. Buy it as early as possible—older people and those with chronic illnesses pay sharply higher rates for life insurance. But don't lie about your health to get a better rate. If the insurance company finds out, it could refund your premiums instead of paying the claims.

HOW MUCH COVERAGE DO YOU NEED?

You need life insurance as long as there is someone in your family who depends on your income. You may need up to 6 to 10 times your annual salary in life insurance. It sounds like a lot, but if your goal is to make sure your loved ones can live as comfortably in the future as they do today, you don't want to short-change them. You can determine how much you need by figuring out what amount of money it would take to make sure your dependents (your spouse, children, elderly parents, or others) can continue to live in their current lifestyle if you die. If you and your spouse work, you should each do separate calculations. Also consider how much coverage your dependents would need if you and your spouse die within a short time of each other.

To calculate exactly how much life insurance you'll need, or at least to get a ballpark figure, you'll need to take into account your spouse's annual expenses (including the mortgage, utilities, and other payments that you currently share) and your children's annual expenses (including child care, nursery school, private and secondary education as well as college expenses). Include at least three months' worth of expenses for an emergency fund—and even more if you want to leave your spouse an extra cushion. Don't forget to add funeral costs. Funerals are a big expense. The National Association of Funeral Directors estimates that the average cost of a funeral was about $6,500 in 2004, but the *actual* cost can top $10,000 after buying the burial plot, flowers, etc.

Next, consider your assets. Your spouse's after-tax income, your yearly Social Security benefits, assets that are currently available (including stocks, bonds, savings, 401[k] distributions, and annuities), as well as life insurance that you already own. Keep in mind if the bulk of your insurance is from your employer, you will lose that benefit if you leave your job. So do your calculations two ways—one with that insurance and one without. There are many Web sites available that can give you a rough estimate of how much life insurance you will need. One of my favorites is the Life Insurance Worksheet at *www.smartmoney.com.* See the "Life Insurance Worksheet" at the end of the book. Also try calculators at insurance Web sites, like *www.accuquote.com* and *www.insweb.com.*

WHO OWNS THE LIFE INSURANCE POLICY?

The person or trust that applies for the policy is considered the *policy owner.* The *insured* is the person whose life is being insured and the *beneficiary* is the person or trust that receives the money when you die. These are important distinctions for estate planning purposes because if you are the owner of your own policy, the money will be considered part of your estate and will determine your estate tax liability. Also, even though you may want your kids to be the beneficiaries to pay for their private school, guitar lessons or camp, minor children cannot be legal beneficiaries. So create a trust to manage the funds on behalf of your children, name the trustees, and leave instructions as to how the money should be spent on their behalf.

PICKING THE RIGHT KIND OF INSURANCE

There are several different types of life insurance policies, but they basically fall into two camps: (1) term insurance and (2) permanent coverage (also known as cash value policies), which includes whole life, universal, and variable insurance.

• *Term insurance.* As the name implies, term insurance covers a specific term, say 5, 10, 20, or 30 years. If you die during that time, your beneficiary gets a death benefit. Term is the simplest and cheapest life insurance you can get and works best for most people.

When it comes to term insurance, you also have some options: *Renewable term* lets you renew the policy (usually at a higher rate) for another period when the term ends. For young couples, annual renewable term, known as ART, which is purchased year by year, may be the cheapest way to go—with premiums as low as a few hundred dollars per year for $250,000 worth of coverage. If you choose renewable term, check periodically to see if premium prices have fallen. If you're healthy, you may be able to switch to a lower rate. *Level term* means your premium stays the same over the life of the term policy, whether rates rise or fall. Premiums are somewhat higher but stay fixed for anywhere from 5 to 30 years depending on the term.

Even though term life insurance is cheap, don't skimp. Rates are so low that you should be able to afford a life insurance policy that will cover your needs. You want to be covered for as long as it takes for your kids to graduate from college or for your retirement income to kick in or until you finish paying off your mortgage, whatever your ultimate goal.

- *Whole life insurance.* Whole life insurance is a permanent policy that stays with you until you die. These polices offer a death benefit and an alternative *cash value* or savings account. The added investment component allows you to build cash value that you can borrow against, withdraw, or use to pay future premiums while you are living. The money in these cash value accounts grows tax-deferred in fixed income investments or mutual funds. Because of the investment potential of cash value policies, the initial premiums are significantly higher than for term insurance.

If you're a conservative investor and have trouble saving, a traditional whole life policy may work for you. You're buying a policy that pays a stated, fixed amount on your death and part of your premium goes toward building cash value from investments that are made by the insurance company. So it can be a great way to force you to save. The idea is that the cash value—the extra cash you contribute beyond what the premium would be for a basic term policy—will grow based on the return on your investments. These plans are marketed as a great investment vehicle because the cash value builds tax-free each year that you keep the policy. Plus, you can borrow against the cash that you've accumulated without being taxed. Your premiums are usually fixed throughout the life of the policy.

There are a couple different types of whole life insurance policies:

- *Universal life insurance* combines term insurance with a money market–type investment that pays a certain rate of return. Universal policies earn interest at the credited interest rate determined each year. This type of whole life policy offers the maximum guaranteed premiums and the minimum guaranteed cash values and death benefits.

- *Variable life insurance* is a whole life policy with an investment fund that is tied to stock or bond mutual fund investments. Since returns fluctuate with the market, this type of insurance has the fewest number of guarantees, but also offers the greatest potential for increases in the cash value. There are required guaranteed annual premiums and a guaranteed minimum death benefit. But there is no guaranteed cash value and you have to select the investments. The mutual fund accounts you can choose from may range from money market to fixed income and aggressive growth funds. Keep in mind, the returns quoted by your insurance agent are estimates—they're not guarantees. Research the investments your broker suggests on your own as well. Remember, if these investments perform poorly, the cash value in your policy could be less than the contributions you've put into it.

That's why life insurance should never be purchased solely as an investment. Your main goal is to protect your loved ones upon your death and make sure they have adequate coverage to cover their needs, not buy products that simply result in large commissions for the insurance broker.

TERM INSURANCE VERSUS CASH VALUE POLICIES

Many people argue that you should always "buy term and invest the difference," but it really depends on how long you intend to keep the policy. If you keep the permanent life policy long enough, that may be a good deal. But "long enough" varies depending on your age, health, insurance company, types of policies chosen, and interest and dividend rates.

The argument against term has been that it pays for only one year of coverage at a time, while cash value allows you to invest additional money. Also, term insurance premium costs can rise each year as you grow older and your chance of dying statistically increases. But now with 20- and 30-year level-term policies, you can lock in an annual premium that never rises. By the time your 30-year level-term policy ends, your children will have finished college, and you'll have built up enough cash in retirement accounts to cover your needs.

Keep in mind that cash value policies can cost between 4 and 15 times as much as term insurance. High fees and commissions are built into these whole life plans as well as surrender charges, if you want to cancel the policy. You'll need to hold on to cash value plans for a while—say 10 years or more—so that you're not hit with heavy early surrender charges. If your investments are poor performers, you still may be left with little or no cash value 5, 10, or even 15 years after you've bought the policy.

So for most young families buying term is the cheapest and least risky way to get the most coverage. In fact, most couples are probably better off buying term and using the money they save on premiums to invest in other tax-deferred vehicles such as IRAs, 401(k)s, or 529 college savings plans. That way you can still save on taxes, but pay far less in commissions and get much higher yields.

Cash value policies still may make the most sense for people who have already maxed out their savings in other tax-deferred accounts. But those families may want to cover their basic insurance needs, the money they need to protect their families, with cheaper term life insurance. If you do buy a cash value policy, make big payments upfront so that you start amassing earnings faster. Also look for low-load policies—policies with low fees and commissions—such as those offered by TIAA-CREF, and USAA.

Before making a final decision, go to some of the insurance Web sites or call a few companies to compare the rates for a term versus cash value policy. You may find a huge difference.

Life insurance rates have come down over the past few years, so you may want to double-check the rates even if you already have a term policy. Start by looking for quotes online. So that you don't get swindled by sites that simply try to get you to use one of their agents, log onto one of the five Web sites recommended by the Consumer Federation of America: *www.accuquote. com, www.insweb.com, www.quotesmith.com, www.term4sale.com,* or *www. youdecide.com. TrustedChoice.com,* a Web site run by the independent Insurance Agents and Brokers of America is another good site. Once you've compared the premiums, check the financial rating of the insurer. You can find ratings at *www.ambest.com, www.fitchratings.com, www.moodys.com,* and *www.standardandpoors.com.*

WHERE TO BUY IT

To avoid dealing with insurance brokers and agents who have a vested interest in selling you a certain type of life insurance policy, you may want to buy it on your own. If you know, for example, that you want a 20-year term policy, you've figured out how much you need and your estate is likely to be exempt from federal estate taxes (under $2 million in 2007), then you could probably buy a policy yourself directly from the company. However, if you're trying to lessen your tax bite and life insurance is an integral part of your estate plan, you probably want to go with a pro.

If you decide you need professional help, look for someone with at least five years' experience. Also, make sure your insurance agent or financial planner has the right credentials, either a CFP (certified financial planner), CLU (chartered life underwriter), ChFC (chartered financial consultant), CPA (certified public accountant), or a law degree (JD or LLM). Insurance agents should be a CLU or ChFC and licensed in the state where you live. Also find out how they're getting paid. Some work on commission; they make money only if you buy a product and therefore often go for the hard sell. Fee-based planners charge a fee and also receive a commission on products they sell, whereas fee-only planners charge a fee for advising you but don't sell any products.

Make sure you check the rating of the company that holds the policy and beware any adviser who says they know more about the insurance company than the ratings agencies.

HEALTHY LIFESTYLE, CHEAPER RATES

To buy a life insurance policy, you have to take a physical. My husband and I found this one of the most disconcerting parts of the process. When we bought our initial policies, this older man cloaked in a tattered tan trench coat arrived at the door of our Manhattan apartment with a battered black plastic briefcase and declared he would need to take some blood samples. It was like something out of a bad horror movie. However, as apprehensive as we were about this stranger coming to take our blood, the tests turned out well and we qualified for preferred (the least expensive) rates. We were lucky. We didn't even realize how important our healthy lifestyle would be to our insurance. We don't smoke, drink much coffee, or consume much alcohol—my husband doesn't drink at all. We eat chicken more than red meat and, at the time, we both exercised regularly.

SHOP AROUND FOR BEST RATES AND RATINGS

When it comes to getting the least expensive life insurance, it pays to eat right, exercise, not drink or smoke, and generally take good care of your body. (Smokers may pay as much as 80% more for the same amount of coverage. But if you quit and don't smoke for at least one year, you may qualify for a lower rate from some insurers.) The cheapest, "preferred" rates go to those applicants in the best health. You should qualify for those rates if you don't smoke, you have a low cholesterol count (under 250) and low blood pressure (140 over 90 or lower), and you're a healthy weight (under 210 pounds for a 5-foot-10-inch man; 175 pounds for a 5-4 woman). By the way, women with comparable health and risk factors typically pay at least 10% less than men for their policies—since they generally live longer than men.

Insurers are most concerned with your cholesterol levels (a predictor of heart disease) and blood-sugar scores (a sign of potential diabetes). It's incredible how much your short-term diet and exercise regime can skew the results. Blood-sugar levels, for example, can increase by up to 50% depending on what you just ate. A slight change could result in a more expensive rate. Some tips: Avoid a steak dinner and other high-salt and -cholesterol foods for 24 hours before the exam. Keep sugar and caffeine out of your system. Don't consume anything other than water for at least 8 hours before the physical. Also, forgo strenuous exercise for at least 24 hours.

If you've fasted and find your cholesterol levels and other test scores are still sky-high, it may be worth double-checking the results with your own doctor just to make sure the lab didn't make a mistake. A higher score can cost you hundreds of dollars more in premiums than you'd expected.

GETTING OUT OF AN EXISTING POLICY

To get out of a term policy, all you have to do is stop paying premiums. Dumping a variable or universal life policy is more complicated. That nasty surrender charge can deplete whatever cash value you've built up. Fees range from one year's premium to as high as 10% of the policy's payoff value—and that surrender charge may be in effect 10 to 20 years after you've bought the policy. If you want out after just a year or two in the policy, you'll lose only the premiums you've already paid. After that, you're probably better off keeping the policy for a while. But see if you can reduce your premiums by paying the minimum amount necessary to pay for mortality costs and administration expenses. If you want an expert analysis, submit your plan

INSURANCE FOR THE CHRONICALLY ILL

Buying life insurance (or disability or long-term care coverage) can be a huge challenge for those with a chronic medical condition. But if you suffer from diabetes, heart disease, or some other illness that can be treated, you may be able to find insurers that will cover you. Though you'll usually pay more, you can keep your premiums down by purchasing insurance from your employer. You'll get group rates, plus you may not be subject to medical underwriting to qualify. If you can't get coverage from your employer, start checking quotes online. Go to InsWeb.com (*www.insweb.com*), which quotes fewer insurers than some of the other sites, but asks for more extensive data, so the prices should more accurately reflect what you'll pay. Some insurers like TIAA-CREF, Allstate, and New York Life don't make their prices available on quote Web sites. So it is worth calling around.

You can also try getting coverage through an impaired-risk insurance agency. It locates companies that sell insurance for people with chronic conditions. Contact the Life and Health Insurance Foundation for Education (www.life-line.org, 202-464-5000) for advice on finding an agency or insurer that covers people with your condition. Also, to help reduce your premiums, document any improvements in your health and ask about special insurance products, such as a death benefit that increases the longer you live. If you can't afford the premiums, get a less expensive policy with a smaller death benefit. You could take out a $50,000 or $75,000 term policy instead of one for $200,000. When your health improves, you can shop for better coverage.

to the Consumer Federation of America (*www.evaluatelifeinsurance.org* or *www.consumerfed.org*), and for $55 to $75 its analysts will walk you through the surrender decision.

Also, ask an independent insurance agent if a maneuver called a Section 1035 might make sense. This lets you swap the savings in your current policy for a cheaper one, or for an annuity. In some cases, the move is tax-free.

HOMEOWNERS INSURANCE

Your home is your castle, but many couples don't invest in the proper financial moat to protect it. One out of every three homes nationwide is underinsured, according to a 2005 survey by Trusted Choice, a group of independent insurance and financial firms. At least 8 million U.S. households own home insurance policies that aren't adequate for their needs. The latest survey showed the typical homeowner was underinsured by 21%. A major reason many homes are underinsured is that owners fail to report improvements to their insurers. Among homeowners who said they significantly remodeled their homes in the last two years, nearly 40% had not updated their homeowners policies, according to Trusted Choice. After remodeling, you may need to increase the policy limit of liability—the amount the insurer would pay if the home were totally destroyed—to reflect the additional value.

VALUE YOUR HOME

Unless you have enough cash on hand to completely rebuild and refurnish your home or apartment, you need a home insurance or renters insurance policy and it needs to reflect the cost of rebuilding your home *today*—with the home improvements that you may have done. When it comes to a homeowners policy, you want to buy enough coverage to cover the cost of rebuilding—don't just rely on the purchase price or appraisal value as a guide. The purchase price may be higher or lower than the cost to rebuild your home, depending on the real estate market in your community. Remember that you don't need to insure the land on which your home is built. That will remain even if the house does not. The land may represent a significant portion of the purchase price, again depending on where you live and how much land you have. A local contractor or appraiser should be able to help you figure out the average cost per square foot to rebuild in your area.

GET PROPER COVERAGE

You still may not be able to get insurance to cover all your rebuilding costs in the event of a widespread disaster. When there is a hurricane or earthquake, everyone with a damaged home wants to hire a contractor to rebuild at the same time. The increased demand for skilled labor and building materials can push up rebuilding costs considerably. Unfortunately, home insurance policies cover less of this "demand surge" than they did several years ago. Finding "guaranteed replacement" coverage is tough. Instead of

---

 RENTERS INSURANCE

Renters insurance is pretty simple and not very expensive. Renters insurance usually costs only $15 to $20 a month, on average. Yet Trusted Choice says about two-thirds of renters don't have it. It covers your belongings against perils such as fire, theft, windstorm, hail, explosion, vandalism, and riots. It also provides personal liability coverage for damage that you, your spouse, or your dependents cause to others. And it provides additional living expenses, known as *loss-of-use coverage*, if you and your family have to move while your apartment is being repaired. Some policies can also cover improvements to your property. As with homeowners insurance, you should aim to cover your possessions for their replacement value, in the event of a loss instead of the actual cash value, which reduces the amount you'll be paid to take account of depreciation.

offering to rebuild your home no matter the cost, most insurers now cap the amount they will pay at 120% of your policy's stated coverage.*

Homeowners policies also usually limit the replacement of your belongings to between 50 and 75% of the home's value. Make a list of your home's contents for a more exact estimate of your needs. (You'll already have a written record if you need to file a claim.) Also, if it's not built into your policy, ask for replacement cost coverage for your home's contents. Otherwise you'll end up with just the depreciated value of any object that is damaged or stolen. Coverage that takes depreciation into account is often called the "actual cash value" average. In addition, consider the impact of inflation over time. Most of the major homeowners insurers include an "inflation guard" feature in their policies that automatically adjusts the homeowners insurance policy's limit each year to take account of inflation in homebuilding costs and contents replacement.

TYPES OF HOMEOWNERS INSURANCE

Here's a list of different types of homeowners policies and events, or *perils,* you are covered for. Read your policy carefully; if a peril isn't listed it means you are not covered.

> **HO-1.** Basic homeowners. Covers your dwelling and personal property against losses from 11 types of perils: fire or lightning; windstorm or hail; explosion; riot or civil commotion; aircraft; vehicles; smoke; vandalism or malicious mischief; theft; damage by glass or safety glazing material that is part of a building; and volcanic eruption.
>
> **HO-2.** Basic homeowners plus. Covers dwelling and personal property against 11 perils plus 6 more: falling objects; weight of ice, snow, or

---

* "Why 2 Out of 3 Homes Are Underinsured," by Liz Pulliam Weston, *MSNMoney.com.*

sleet; three categories of water-related damage from home utilities or appliances; and electrical surge damage.

HO-3. Extended or special homeowners. Covers 17 stated perils plus any other peril *not* specified in your policy, except for flood, earthquake, war, and nuclear accident. Most homes are covered by HO-3 type policies.

HO-4. Renters coverage. Covers only personal property from 17 listed perils.

HO-5. All-risk coverage for building and personal property. This policy form isn't sold very often anymore.

HO-6. Condominium coverage. Covers personal property from 17 listed perils along with certain building items in which the unit owner might have an insurance interest.

HO-7. For mobile home owners.

HO-8. Basic older home. Covers dwelling and personal property from 11 perils. Differs from HO-1 in that it covers repairs or actual cash values—not rebuilding costs. This is for homes where in the event of a loss the rebuilding of some historic or architectural aspects would make the home's replacement cost significantly higher than its market value.

You can buy homeowners insurance with coverage for either the actual cash value of your belongings, or for their replacement cost. With a cash value policy, the insurance company deducts a certain amount for depreciation from the cash value of your belongings. That means you may get only $1,500 to replace your $2,000 sofa under a cash value policy. With a replacement policy, you'd get the actual replacement cost of the sofa if it was damaged or destroyed. The best insurers ask a lot of detailed questions about the features of your home to determine how much insurance you should have. Some insurance firms rely on less effective methods, such as multiplying the home's square footage by average construction costs in the area, but the cost to rebuild *your* home could be much more than that.

ADDITIONAL COVERAGE

To make sure you are adequately insured, you may want to add the following options or coverage as well:

- *inflation guard clause:* This option automatically adjusts the coverage limit on the home each time the policy is renewed to reflect current construction costs.
- *ordinance-and-law coverage:* If you have an older home, you may also want to consider adding *upgrade coverage* to bring it up to current codes—and those costs typically aren't covered in the standard replacement policy.
- *umbrella liability coverage:* Your homeowners policy protects you against lawsuits for accidents that happen on your property. It also covers you if your dog bites someone. But you may want to get a personal umbrella policy for additional coverage over and above your regular homeowners liability limits.
- *home business coverage:* If you have office equipment (computers, scanners, fax machines) that is worth more than $2,500 in the home, buy a rider or separate policy to cover your "business property."
- *riders:* If you have expensive jewelry, antiques, and collectables, or a lot of computers and other home office equipment, you may need to get extra coverage through a rider, known as a *personal articles policy.* Also, consider "scheduled" coverage for a diamond ring, other jewelry, or art that can increase in value over time. Be sure to get your valuables reappraised periodically to keep the scheduled amounts up-to-date to reflect the actual replacement costs.
- *flood insurance:* Standard home-insurance policies don't cover

flooding, but the federal government does through the National Flood Insurance Program. It's not only good protection for coastal homes; the Insurance Information Institute says about 25% of all claims that are paid after a flood are in areas that are not designated high-risk for flooding.

You'll also have to pick a deductible. As with all insurance policies, the higher your deductible—the more you pay out-of-pocket—the more you save on premiums. However, if you live in an area vulnerable to hurricanes or hailstorms, your deductible for storm-related losses may be subject to a percentage deductible rather than the typical dollar deductible, raising the amount you would pay out-of-pocket before the policy kicks in. In some

 TAKE STOCK OF WHAT YOU'VE GOT

Having an up-to-date home inventory will help you get your insurance claim settled faster, verify losses for your income tax return, and help you purchase the correct amount of insurance. So take stock of what you've got.

• Make a list of your possessions (note where you bought each item and the make and model).

• Clip sales receipts, purchase contracts, and appraisals for these items to the list.

• Take a picture or videotape each item.

• Store list, photos, and/or videotape in safe deposit box or at a friend's or relative's home.

For free software to make a home inventory, go to *www.knowyourstuff.org.*

SOURCE: Insurance Information Institute.

coastal areas, for example, you may have a hurricane or windstorm deductible based on a percentage of your home's value, usually 1% to 5% instead of a flat $500 to $1,000 deductible. So, if you have insured your $300,000 home with a policy that has a 2% deductible for any qualifying wind event, your out-of-pocket costs would be $6,000.

WAYS TO SAVE ON HOME INSURANCE

You can save money by buying less insurance (not recommended) or applying for more discounts.

1. Most experts advise purchasing insurance coverage that provides a minimum of 80% of the replacement cost of your home and your belongings—but you should really try to get 100% if you can.
2. Getting your home and auto insurance from the same company may help you keep your premiums down.
3. Boosting your deductible can also trim costs. If your homeowners and auto insurance policies don't provide adequate protection, you may need to buy a personal or "umbrella" liability policy.
4. Don't put in too many claims. Frequent claims are red flags for insurers. So tap into your emergency reserve if you have to and try to cover claims under $1,000.
5. Using deadbolt locks, burglar alarms, smoke detectors, and other items that improve security and safety can also bring discounts.

Whether it is your life or your home, you need to be properly insured to protect your assets and those that you intend to leave to your family. This is often a part of the picture that many couples fail to assess and fund as fully as they should. A recent survey found 32 million Americans don't have the right kind of insurance. If you don't have the right kind of insurance for your home, you will never be able to rebuild it to close to its current condition. And think about how your spouse or children will remember you if you decide to get a new Mercedes-Benz every few years instead of buying adequate life insurance. Don't skimp. You have more than your own life to consider.

8

GOOD WILL HUNTING

*Draft an Estate Plan So You Can Share
Your Wealth with Others.*

The ambulance pulls up with a husband, wife, father, or mother. Miguel, an emergency room physician, knows this person is not going to make it. But the injury isn't just physical—it's economic as well. All too often, he sees the personal and financial devastation families go through when a loved one dies. Miguel told me he did not want his wife and young son to go through the same heart-wrenching, emotionally draining experience. So after their son's third birthday, Miguel and his wife decided to start doing some research on wills, trusts, and other aspects of estate planning. They met with a financial adviser to come up with a plan. "We wanted to minimize our tax liability, leave more to our son, but we also wanted to make sure that our wishes were known, that if we're not around, that there's somebody to care for our son," Miguel remembers. Now that they have an estate plan in place, he is relieved. "You know, you hope for the best, but you have to plan for the worst."

Preparing for the worst is certainly not a pleasant thought, which is why most of us put off planning for our own demise—or worse, the death of a spouse. Most couples are focused on making money so that they can pay the mortgage and other bills, also save for their own retirement and college for their kids, and hopefully have a little left over for a summer vacation. Who has the time to think about who will handle our financial affairs and make medical decisions if we are unable to do so? If we're dead, we won't know the difference, so why should we care?

Well, you *should* care a great deal. You've worked hard to build your assets—your home, your savings, other investments, and personal property— and to provide a level of financial security for your loved ones. If *you* don't make some provisions, decisions about your assets and your heirs, even your medical care, if you become disabled or incapacitated, those decisions may be made by your state or by a complete stranger. Or they may be made by a relative we all know too well—Uncle Sam. "Everyone has an estate plan; some are voluntary and some are involuntary." says Ivory Johnson, director of financial planning at the Scarborough Group, "The fact is that if couples don't predetermine who gets what, when they get it, and how they get it, somebody else will do it for them."

Not to mention that without an estate plan, your taxes and accountant's and attorney's fees could, in some cases, cut the value of your estate nearly in half. Another wrinkle: the distribution of your assets could be delayed at a time when your family members and others need them most. The reality—as morbid as it sounds—is that you're probably worth more dead than alive. So protecting, preserving, and managing the wealth you've accumulated and the wealth you're likely to amass in the future is as important as making money today. That's the primary goal of estate planning.

Yet fewer than half of adults and even a smaller percentage of those with children have a will. Many couples believe devising an estate plan will be too daunting, too time-consuming, and too complex. Or, they think they are too young or don't have enough money to bother having even a basic will. Your age or your assets shouldn't be the determining factor. No matter how old you are or what you own, you should ask yourself, Do I want control of where my assets eventually go, or do I want the state to decide for me? If you want control, you need to start doing some estate planning. Yet, even the well-to-do aren't doing estate planning. A Charles Schwab survey conducted a few years ago found that one in four affluent Americans have no estate plan, though the average net worth of those surveyed was $1.7 million!

Sure, if your net worth falls under the $2 million per person federal estate-tax threshold, you probably won't have to worry about *federal* estate taxes, although states have their own estate taxes and you could take a hit there. The amount of income that's free from federal estate taxes goes up again, to $3.5 million, in 2009, under the Economic Growth and Tax Relief Reconciliation Act of 2001. But then, the federal estate tax is set to be repealed in 2010. Don't get too excited. It probably won't go away for long. Unless Congress decides to make the repeal permanent, the estate tax will rise from the dead a year later, reverting back to the 2001 rate of $1 million.

Even if you don't think you're rich enough to have to worry about an estate plan, you may be richer than you think. Don't just focus on your paycheck—think about your property. Consider your entire net worth. See the "Net Worth Worksheet for Estate Plan" at the end of the book. Write down of all of your assets—life insurance benefits, your retirement accounts, your home, as well as other investments. What's your tally? You'll probably find your estate quickly adds up and may exceed the federal estate tax threshold that currently keeps those assets out of Uncle Sam's hands. If your assets do exceed the federal estate tax threshold—as it stands now or what it may be after 2011—you may want to talk to a financial adviser or estate planning attorney, who can help you with more sophisticated estate tax planning.

Yet for most couples, the bulk of estate planning has nothing to do with taxes. The basic goal is to protect your assets by making sure they are distributed according to your wishes when you die. You also want to ensure that you, not the state, will choose the person who will manage your medical and financial affairs if you become incapacitated. And of most importance to couples, like Miguel and his wife, you want a plan that protects and provides for your children.

How to Get Started

Setting up an estate plan doesn't have to be complicated, time-consuming, or costly. Rande Spiegelman, vice president of financial planning at Charles Schwab, suggests you start by simply reviewing the beneficiaries of your insurance policies and retirement accounts and updating them to reflect your recent marriage, birth of a child, death of a relative, or some other event. Paying attention to how your property is owned is critical. Say you designated your first spouse to get your life insurance proceeds and then forgot to change that designation when you remarried. Even if you say explicitly in your will that you want to leave all of your assets to Spouse No. 2, the insurance money still goes to Spouse No. 1 because that is who is on your beneficiary designation form.

You may want to add one or more of your heirs as a co-owner on your home, or bank or brokerage account. The beneficiaries here may also supersede a will. This means that often, upon the death of the first joint owner of the account, the survivor will receive all the proceeds, no matter what the will says. Still, if you really want to make sure that your wishes are carried out, you'll need to draft a will (which you could do on your own or hire an estate planning attorney). You may also want to establish trusts, which should be done by an estate planning attorney. But to cut down on the time and expense it will take to meet with a professional, make sure you know what you have and what you want to protect.

So first, *take inventory of your assets and liabilities.* Before you can figure out who should get what, you need to figure out what you have and what you owe. Once you start to calculate all that you've accumulated, you'll probably have a better idea of how you want your assets distributed.

- *Property*: Write down the value of your home and other real estate, cars, jewelry, artwork, and other physical assets, including expensive cameras, computers, furniture, and other household items. You'll want to jot down the market price of your home: what your house is worth, not how much equity you have built. Also, when it comes to vehicles, don't worry about car loans you may have. You want to figure out the Blue Book values of the cars that you own. And when it comes to furniture and other personal property, you want to figure out the amount you would get for all of your stuff if you had to sell it today.

• *Savings and investments:* Add up the value of all 401(k) plans, IRAs, and other retirement accounts. Find recent statements from each of your banks, and from investment and brokerage accounts. If you own any U.S. savings bonds, go to the bank and find out exactly how much they are worth.

• *Life insurance:* Make a list of all life insurance policies, including the cash value and death benefit.

• *Liabilities:* Write down all liabilities, including mortgage balance, home equity loans and lines of credit, car loans, college loans, credit card debt, and any other loans or debts.

Next, *define your estate planning objectives.* If you decide to meet with an estate planning attorney, you can save yourself time and money by coming up with answers to important questions ahead of time. Rande Spiegelman suggests asking yourself six questions:

1. Who will get your assets when you die? How will you decide on the proportions of the stock?
2. If the beneficiaries aren't living at the time of your death, who will you name as successor beneficiaries?
3. If you have minor children, who do you want to care for them?
4. What assets do you want to put aside to provide for your children's ongoing care and education?
5. Who will manage your affairs if you become disabled, and who will distribute your assets upon your death?
6. Who will make decisions on your behalf if you become incapacitated?

INSURING GOOD WILL

Wills are the most basic documents for estate planning. You'd probably rather determine the fate of your estate than leave it up to some government bureaucrat. Your will spells out exactly who gets what—including your children—and names an executor to carry out your wishes. Without a will, the laws of the state allow it to divvy up your assets according to its statutes and it can also decide who becomes responsible for your kids. Say both you and your spouse die in a car accident; without a will, your children become wards of the state and typically the court will pick which of your family members will get to raise them. A scary thought that would have me dialing a financial adviser or estate planning attorney immediately!

Even if you don't have children, you and your spouse should each have a will. Otherwise the state will follow a basic plan to determine how to divide your assets and it probably won't be the way that you desired. For example, without a will in most states, a surviving spouse gets only one-third to one-half of an estate. The state decides who gets the rest. Without a will, states don't generally give anything to stepchildren you haven't adopted or charities you want to support. Friends get zilch. And the portion of your estate that goes to your kids will be paid to them outright, usually at age 18, rather than held in trust until you want them to have it.

Also without a will, it could take a lot longer for your assets to get to your heirs, as the state wrangles with "interested parties" over what to do with it. So when it comes to dividing assets in the will, be as specific as possible. If you want to make sure an heirloom silver tea set, painting, or piece of jewelry or furniture goes to a certain child, relative, friend, or charity, put it in writing.

A will allows you to call the shots. But only assets in your own name solely (or your share of community property in Arizona, California, Idaho, Lousiana, Nevada, New Mexico, Texas, Washington, and Wisconsin) fall under a will's jurisdiction. Keep in mind, however, that many assets won't pass to your beneficiaries with only a will. For example, if you and your spouse own your home or investment accounts jointly with right of survivorship, they automatically go to the survivor. Life insurance death benefits, balances in retirement accounts (such as IRAs, 401(k)s, and pension plans), money in bank and brokerage accounts, usually automatically pass to the listed beneficiary. You still need a will, though, for everything else you own. You also definitely need a will to name a guardian for your children and to decide who gets what in the event that you both die at the same time.

Executor: If you have a will, the executor will ultimately be responsible for settling your estate, including taking inventory, appraising and distributing assets, paying taxes, and settling your debts. Your estate planning attorney, accountant, or financial adviser can serve in that role. If your estate is small, you may choose to appoint a spouse, adult child, relative, or friend as executor.

Guardian: Choosing a guardian can often be a contentious discussion among some couples. You may not think your husband's 40-year-old brother, who hasn't stopped "playing the field," is the wisest choice to become a family man. Your husband may not be thrilled with the idea of your sister, who is still in college but is thinking of taking time off to work on a fishing boat off the coast of Guatemala, taking on the responsibility of raising your toddlers. One solution is to pick two guardians—a first choice and a second, in case something unexpected happens. Suppose you name your sister, and later she gets married and then divorced. She has her own kids and may not be in a position to take your child or children. It's good to have a fallback plan. Your brother-in-law may have matured by this point and wouldn't be such a bad choice after all.

You could also split responsibilities among your siblings or other relatives or friends. You may decide that one relative is more nurturing and would be a better guardian, while the other is very organized and adept at handling financial matters. That's the decision my husband and I made; our estate planning attorney suggested we compromise: give one spouse's sibling financial guardianship by allowing him or her to act as trustee (overseeing the investment and distribution of the assets) and the other's sibling personal guardianship. That's exactly what we did and it was amazing how quickly that compromise cleared any tension between us.

DO-IT-YOURSELF WILLS

You can definitely draft a simple will yourself. There are plenty of books, computer software programs, and Web sites that offer standard will forms. Just make sure you find out the specific requirements of your local jurisdiction when it comes to the number and residence of witnesses, notaries, etc. One well-regarded software program, Quicken WillMaker (by Nolo), *www.nolo.com,* costs about $50. But if you have a large estate or anything complicated, it's probably best to hire an estate planning attorney. The cost can range between $500 for a simple will to $3,000 for wills involving basic estate-tax planning.

DON'T LIVE WITHOUT THEM: THREE ESSENTIAL LEGAL DOCUMENTS

Unless you want a stranger making critical decisions about who will pay your bills when you are incapacitated or whether to shut off the respirator that keeps you alive, there are three legal documents that are just as important to your estate plan, if not more so, than a will.

• **Durable power of attorney for finances**—assigns someone, called an "attorney-in-fact," to handle your finances (including paying bills, depositing checks, and carrying out other routine transactions) if you are unable to do so. You can write into the document as much or as little power as you'd like.

- **Durable power of attorney for health care or health care proxy**—designates someone to handle your medical decisions if you are ill and can't make health care decisions for yourself.
- **Living will**—states whether you want extraordinary means used to prolong your life when you're critically ill and tells doctors what kind of care you want (including whether or not you wish to be kept alive by life support) if you should become terminally ill and incapacitated. (Some states combine the living will and durable power of attorney in one form, known as an advanced medical directive.)

Having these forms can eliminate much of the pain—and sometimes great expense—on the part of your heirs. Marcia had to spend $5,000—a considerable slice of her salary as a schoolteacher in White Plains, New York—to hire a lawyer and file to become her mother's guardian. Her mother had a stroke and needed to go into a nursing home. Although she had an up-to-date will, her mother never signed a durable power of attorney for her finances. So Marcia couldn't get access to her mother's assets to cover nursing home bills until she got the legal authority.

When it comes to medical decisions, having a living will and health care proxy or durable power of attorney for health care can truly be a matter of life or death. The U.S. Supreme Court has ruled that every individual has the right to direct his or her own medical care, even if a spouse, parent, or other relative disagrees with those directions. But without those documents, consider the potential legal wrangling and emotional toll that could ensue for your loved ones.

You and your spouse should take the time to think about what to do if you are incapacitated. Do you want to be on a respirator? Do you want to be fed food and water through tubing systems? Do you want pain medication? Do you want to be cared for at home or in the hospital?

Also, who do you want to help make these decisions for you? Your spouse is probably the logical choice for your heath care proxy or durable power of attorney for health care to make decisions about your health care as well as your finances. But you still need to have a fallback plan in case both of you are injured and incapacitated, or killed. Consider choosing someone who lives nearby for the health care proxy so that they can travel to or from the hospital or stay with you for an extended period of time. The person who handles your finances doesn't necessarily have to live close by, although you may still want to pick someone who lives nearby in case they'll have to sell your home or need to be in close proximity to your bank.

ESTATE TAX PLANNING: AVOIDING UNCLE SAM

Estate taxes may never go away permanently. As discussed, the federal estate tax is scheduled to disappear in 2010, but state estate taxes will remain. Planning ahead, any couple that thinks that together they will have more than $2 million to pass along should consider these strategies to avoid paying federal estate taxes. Setting up a trust is more complicated—and more expensive—than drafting a will, so you will need to hire an estate planning attorney and it could cost you about $2,000.

Living trust: Many financial advisers advocate setting up a living trust (also called *revocable trust*), which, unlike a will, allows you to house assets while you're alive. However, the merits of these trusts are debatable. On the plus side, they let you avoid probate, which is the legal process in which the state verifies your will, asks for objections to it, and makes sure that bills are paid and assets are properly distributed. In a trust, assets remain private, in case you have property that you do not want to be part of the public record. Also if you own homes in two or more states, they'll each face separate probates, so it can be simpler to put them all in a living trust.

But there are also many downsides to living trusts. They cost a lot more than a simple will—about $1,000 to $5,000 in lawyer's fees plus administrative costs. Keep in mind that some of your assets, like life insurance policies, retirement accounts and a home that is owned jointly with right of survivor-ship, bypass probate anyway. A living trust will be of little help if assets are not properly titled—they have to be retitled into the trust's name. If you're counting on a living trust helping to avoid your state's probate process, you may not need to bother if you're in a state that already has pretty easy proce-dures, like New York or New Jersey. However, Florida, California, and Mas-sachusetts are known for more time-consuming probate. Generally speaking, young couples probably don't need these. But the older you are and the more money you have, the more you may want to consider a revocable trust.

Bypass trust: This type of trust is typically provided for in a will and preserves the estate tax exemption for each spouse even after one dies. Most couples think that just because the IRS generally allows you to give every-thing to your spouse estate tax–free, they don't have to worry about setting up this kind of trust. But if you have a large estate, this so-called unlimited marital deduction simply postpones the inevitable. From 2006 to 2008, for example, each spouse can shelter $2 million from federal estate taxes for a total of $4 million. But if all your property is owned jointly and a spouse dies, one of the two exemptions dies too. However, both exemptions can be preserved if assets are divided, titled separately, and placed into two differ-ent bypass trusts before a spouse's death. When a husband dies, for exam-ple, his estate bypasses his wife's estate. If his trust allows, the wife can live off its income and even its principal. Then when the wife dies, up to $2 mil-lion of his principal and $2 million of hers go to heirs tax-free—preserving the $4 million shelter. Although the money you leave behind may be ear-marked for your kids, your spouse can tap into the trust fund to meet living costs. But since the money technically "bypasses" both of your estates, it never gets hit by federal estate taxes.

QTIP trust: A qualified terminable interest property (QTIP) trust is often used with a bypass trust, in what's called an A-B trust plan. A QTIP trust requires that the surviving spouse receive all the income from the trust for life. It defers the estate tax until the surviving spouse's death. For tax purposes, the value of the QTIP trust's assets goes into your spouse's estate, not yours, even though you designate who gets the trust's assets when your spouse dies. That way you can leave more than $2 million for your kids, but they won't have to pay taxes on the money until your spouse dies.

Here's one way it would work: Say you're worth $3.5 million and your wife is worth $500,000. First you could set up a bypass trust in your will for $2 million, making your kids the ultimate beneficiaries. You'd be free and clear of federal estate taxes, since it's sheltered by your 2007 exemption. But what should you do with the other $1.5 million in your estate? You could leave it to your spouse with no tax penalty (because of the unlimited marital deduction) and she could determine how the money should be spent. Or you could give it to your kids, but they'd have to pay taxes on it immediately. On the other hand, if you set up a QTIP trust and named your kids as beneficiaries of the $1.5 million, the trust's assets are counted as part of your wife's estate for tax purposes. But when she dies, the cash will go where you want it to go. And since she's still under or at the $2 million estate-tax exemption, there's no federal estate tax bill.

Irrevocable life insurance trust: Another popular way to minimize estate taxes is to create an irrevocable life insurance trust, as this trust owns your life insurance policy (or policies). It pays the premiums, collects the death benefits when you die, and distributes the money according to the terms of the trust. Since you don't own the insurance (it's owned by the trust), the proceeds aren't included in your estate. But these trusts have their flaws. Once you set up the trust, the terms cannot be changed. All you can do is stop making premiums so that the insurance will lapse.

STATE ESTATE TAXES

Beth had a single aim when she and her husband, Lou, were making plans about what would happen to their estate when they die. She wanted to designate a guardian for their 13-year-old son, Christopher, and also set up a

trust to make sure he would be financially secure. Beth was confident that
their estate plan prepared them for the worst. Then, her home state of Oregon threw its residents a curveball—as the state inheritance (estate) tax became more expensive. Because they are so focused on the federal estate tax,
few couples realize that federal exemption may not protect your estate from
a steep state estate tax bill when you die.

Although the federal estate tax is set to disappear in 2010, many states
aren't as eager to bury their own death taxes. In the past, most states im-
posed an estate tax that was linked to the federal tax. But many states, including Oregon, Kansas, New York, and Virginia, as well as the District of
Columbia, have recently separated or "decoupled" their estate tax from the
federal system. As a result, families in those states could see their overall
estate tax burden increase substantially.

The tax burden is "particularly acute" for married couples because their
estate plans usually include a bypass trust, which is designed so that no federal estate tax is paid when the first spouse dies, says estate planning attorney
Lawrence Chane of Blank Rome, LLP, in Philadelphia. Unfortunately, this
standard strategy can't shield an estate from the extra state estate tax.

There are ways to rewrite your will or trust to defer the state estate tax,
but you need to make sure that in doing so, your estate won't face a greater
federal tax burden down the road. Beth and Lou put a disclaimer in their
will so that the surviving spouse could delay paying taxes by refusing to accept a portion of the estate. Another approach is to claim a special marital
tax deduction. Giving away enough money to bring the taxable estate below
the federal and state thresholds is also an option. Currently, the law allows
anyone to give anyone else up to $12,000 a year without tax. So a couple can
give $24,000 a year to each child or grandchild tax-free. A final strategy may
be most appealing to northeasterners who've grown tired of the cold win-
ters. If you move to Florida or California you can avoid state taxes since
neither state has separated its tax. The key is to consult with an estate planning attorney to create a plan that has some flexibility.

LETTERS AND RECORDS

Often people leave a will but no information on how to figure out where to find important financial and other information, so spouses and children have to search all over to find out where you've stashed things like computer passwords or alarm codes, or more important, the name, address and phone number of your estate planning attorney and financial adviser. Make sure you leave your loved ones with a list of what they need to know, including who the lawyer is, and how to contact him or her. Let them know where you keep your will, though the attorney should have a copy on file. Keep a list of Social Security numbers, bank and brokerage accounts, retirement accounts, insurance policies, as well as assets and liabilities in a safe-deposit box as long as a third party has access to it. But make sure you leave a note in a desk drawer, or somewhere where your loved ones can easily access it, that says where the safe deposit key is, which bank the box is in, which branch and the box number.

FUNERAL AND BURIAL PLANS

Preparing for the worst also involves dealing with funeral and burial plans. Don't just leave a letter tucked away in your desk with your wishes and assume that your spouse, children, or other family members will find it. Leave a copy of your final letter of instructions with your estate planning attorney so that it can be handed to your executor or your spouse or your children before they make the funeral arrangements.

HELPFUL WEB SITES

The more assets you have, the more complicated your estate plan may be. But there is a lot of information available and knowing what to expect throughout the process should help alleviate your anxiety. If you need a financial adviser that specializes in estate planning, the National Association of Estate Planners & Councils' Web site (*www.naepc.org*) offers a searchable database of accredited estate planners. The American College of Trust and Estate Counsel's Web site (*www.actec.org*) will have a list of estate planning lawyers in your state. The National Network of Estate Planning Attorneys (*www.netplanning.com*) also offers a handful of lawyers who specialize in estate planning in most states. Nolo (*www.nolo.com*) is one of the best self-help legal sites with a great section on Wills & Estate Planning. The National Association of Financial and Estate Planning (*www.nafep.com*) also has good articles. Finally, check out estate planning links on general financial information Web sites, like MSN Money (*moneycentral.msn.com*), CNN Money.com (*money.cnn.com*) and Smartmoney.com (*www.smartmoney.com/estate*).

AFTERWORD

THE BIG PAYOFF

Most people forget their dreams right after they wake up.

The craziest, most colorful dreams make perfect sense when you're asleep. You have wings, you can be on Mars, you can be bouncing across a landscape of marshmallows, and it all seems right and acceptable as long as your eyes are closed. But once the alarm rings, after the cold water from your shower hits your face, the moment you merge with traffic and join the daily commute, whatever you were thinking in the night, whatever visions were running through your head when the lights were out, it all fades away into the mundane, nine-to-five, BlackBerry world of making a dollar. Try to remember the dream you had yesterday—or last week Thursday. You've probably forgotten it already.

Dreams are the farthest things from the minds of most working couples. They're all about reality.

A lot of couples today are facing a financial meltdown. A two-income family typically earns significantly more than the one-income household they were raised in, but they have less in discretionary income. Rising housing costs, skyrocketing health insurance and tuition payments have forced many middle-class families to live paycheck to paycheck.

Harvard Law professor Elizabeth Warren, author of *The Two-Income Trap*, says today's two-income families make 75% more than their one-income parents made a generation ago, but have less money to show for it. Why? Warren says, "I thought it would be a story of overconsumption, of too many trips to the mall, too many Game Boys, too many expensive sneakers." But Warren found today's two-income families are actually spending less on clothing, on food, furniture and appliances than their one-income parents. Instead, it's fixed expenses that are pressing families against the wall. Says Warren: "Families today are spending more than ever on a mortgage, on health insurance, on a second car so that mom can get to work, and on tuition, preschool, sometimes private schools, and college for those who are at the other end of the age spectrum."

The strategies in this book were designed to help couples break out of the cycle of economic dependence and into the sunlight of financial freedom. Liberated from worries, emancipated from monetary stress, couples are free to pursue their true desires.

Having read this book, perhaps now you can think about what you really want.

APPENDICES

Needs vs. Wants Worksheet

(These are just examples. You and your spouse should make a copy of this worksheet and write down your most essential needs and most desired wants.)

NEED	MONTHLY COST	PRIORITY
Mortgage	$2,500	1
Groceries	$ 300	2

Total Cost of Needs _____

WANT	MONTHLY COST	PRIORITY
Annual trip	$100	1
New car	$500	2

Total Cost of Wants _____

- - - - - - - - - - - - - - - - -

Budget Worksheet

MONTHLY INCOME

Paycheck 1   _____

Paycheck 2   _____

Total After-Tax Income   _____

MONTHLY EXPENSES

Committed Expenses

Mortgage/Rent   _____

Insurance—Home   _____

Real Estate Taxes   _____

Phone   _____

Utilities—Gas/Water/Electric _____

Other Household Expenses   _____

Total Household Expenses   _____

Groceries   _____

Clothing/Dry Cleaning   _____

Auto Loan   _____

Insurance—Auto   _____

Gasoline   _____

Other Transportation   _____

Total Food/Clothing/
Transportation Expenses   _____

Insurance—Health/Dental   _____

Insurance—Life   _____

Insurance—Disability   _____

Other Insurance   _____

Education _____

Child care _____

Other committed expenses _____

Total Committed Expenses _____

Discretionary Expenses

Entertainment/Dining _____

Recreation/Travel/Hobbies _____

Charitable Contributions _____

Gifts _____

Home Improvements _____

Miscellaneous Purchases _____

Total Discretionary Expenses _____

TOTAL MONTHLY EXPENSES _____

MONTHLY SAVINGS

401(k) or Employer's Plan _____

IRAs _____

Pensions _____

Other Retirement Savings _____

College Savings _____

Emergency Fund _____

Other Savings _____

TOTAL MONTHLY SAVINGS _____

60% Solution Budget Worksheet

Here's a slimmed down version of the Budget Workout, based on the 60% Solution, devised by MSN Money editor Richard Jenkins. Ideally, he suggests, your committed expenses (including taxes) for the month should equal 60% of your monthly income. Retirement savings, long-term savings, short-term savings, and fun money should each equal 10% of your monthly income. In the end, your total expenditures should equal your total income.

MONTHLY INCOME

Paycheck 1 _____

Paycheck 2 _____

TOTAL _____

MONTHLY EXPENDITURES

Committed Expenses _____
(60% of total monthly income: includes
taxes withheld from pay, as well as health
insurance, mortgage, rent, utilities,
groceries, car loan, all household expenses)

Retirement Savings _____
(10% of total monthly income;
includes 401(k), IRAs, pensions)

Long-Term Savings _____
(10% of total monthly income; includes
college savings, other goals that are more
than 5 years away)

Short-Term Savings   _____

(10% of monthly income; includes

emergency fund for irregular

expenses)

Fun Money   _____

(10% of monthly income; includes

dining out, movies, hobbies

and vacations)

TOTAL EXPENDITURES   _____

(100% of total income)

Retirement Savings Worksheet

	YOU	*SPOUSE*
1. Are you saving for retirement? (Yes/No)	_____	_____
2. In how many years do you plan to retire?	_____	_____
3. What percentage of your gross income do you contribute to retirement savings?	_____	_____
4. Do you participate in an employer-sponsored retirement plan (i.e., 401(k), 403(b,), 457 plans)? (Yes/No)	_____	_____

You:

Type of plan   _____
Company   _____
Balance   _____

Spouse:

Type of plan   _____
Company   _____
Balance   _____

| 5. Total savings in company plan: | $_____ | $_____ |
| 6. Do you have money sitting in a former employer's retirement plan? (Yes/No) | _____ | _____ |

YOU   *SPOUSE*

You:

Type of plan   _____

Company   _____

Balance   _____

Spouse:

Type of plan   _____

Company   _____

Balance   _____

7. Total savings in other company
   plan: $_____ $_____

8. Do you participate in a pension
   plan at work? (Yes/No)   _____   _____

You:

Company   _____

Balance $_____

Spouse:

Company   _____

Balance $_____

9. Total vested value of company
   pension: $_____ $_____

10. Do you participate in other
    retirement plans? (Yes/No)   _____   _____

YOU   *SPOUSE*

(Please list all IRAs, Roth IRAs,
SEP-IRAs, SIMPLE IRA, Solo 401(k)s)

You:
Type of plan   _____
Financial institution   _____
Balance $_____

Type of Plan   _____
Financial institution   _____
Balance $_____

Spouse:
Type of plan   _____
Financial institution   _____
Balance $_____

Type of Plan   _____
Financial institution   _____
Balance $_____

11. Total savings in other retirement plans: $_____ $_____

12. Have you earmarked money
in a taxable account for retirement
savings? (Yes/No)   _____   _____

You:
Type of plan   _____
Financial institution   _____
Balance $_____

	YOU	*SPOUSE*

Spouse:

Type of plan   _____

Financial institution   _____

Balance $_____

13. Total retirement savings in
    taxable account: $_____ $_____

14. TOTAL RETIREMENT SAVINGS
    (Add lines 5, 7, 9, 11, 13) $_____ $_____

Home Buying Worksheet 1

HOW MUCH CAN YOU SPEND?

Use the Budget Workout or 60% Solution Worksheet earlier in this section to
figure out your monthly expenses and then subtract the housing expenses
(rent or mortgage, real estate taxes, home insurance, and utilities). What
remains are your total Monthly Nonhousing Expenses. Then subtract those
expenses from your Total Monthly Income to find out the money you have
available for Housing Expenses.

Take-Home Pay 1	_____
Take-Home Pay 2	_____
Income from Interest and Dividends	_____
Income from Rent or Leases	_____
Other Income	_____
Total Monthly Income	_____
Total Monthly Nonhousing Expenses	_____
Money Available for Housing Expenses	_____

Home Buying Worksheet 2

WHAT IS ON YOUR WISH LIST?

Price Range _____

Maximum Down Payment _____

Maximum Monthly Payment _____

	Must Have	*Would Like*	*Don't Want*
Size			
Total Square Footage	_____	_____	_____
Bedrooms 1 2 3 4 5	_____	_____	_____
Full Bathrooms 1 2 3	_____	_____	_____
Half Bathrooms 1 2 3	_____	_____	_____
Exterior			
Style (Colonial, Contemporary, Split-Level, Ranch, Tudor)	_____	_____	_____
New Roof	_____	_____	_____
Exterior Finish (Brick, Stone, Vinyl Siding, Stucco, Clapboard)	_____	_____	_____
Landscaping	_____	_____	_____
Sidewalks	_____	_____	_____
Paved Driveway	_____	_____	_____
Interior			
Move-In Condition	_____	_____	_____
Fixer Upper	_____	_____	_____
New Carpeting	_____	_____	_____
Hardwood Floors	_____	_____	_____
New Kitchen	_____	_____	_____

	Must Have	*Would Like*	*Don't Want*
Eat-In Kitchen	_____	_____	_____
Pantry	_____	_____	_____
Formal Living Room	_____	_____	_____
Formal Dining Room	_____	_____	_____
Family Room	_____	_____	_____
Fireplace	_____	_____	_____
Laundry Room	_____	_____	_____
Attached Garage	_____	_____	_____
Finished Basement	_____	_____	_____
Finished Attic	_____	_____	_____
Screened Porch	_____	_____	_____
Expansion Possibilities	_____	_____	_____
Other	_____	_____	_____

Heating/Cooling

Type of Heat (Gas, Oil, Electric, Steam)	_____	_____	_____
Central Air Conditioning	_____	_____	_____
Low Energy Costs	_____	_____	_____
Storm Windows	_____	_____	_____
Insulation	_____	_____	_____

Neighborhood

New Construction	_____	_____	_____
Close to Schools	_____	_____	_____
Close to Stores	_____	_____	_____
Close to Public Transportation	_____	_____	_____
Close to Major Roads	_____	_____	_____
Close to Friends/Relatives	_____	_____	_____
Children in Neighborhood	_____	_____	_____
Quiet Street	_____	_____	_____

Health Needs Worksheet

Check the three things that are most important to you in determining health care benefits:

_____ Existing relationship with a doctor or hospital/medical facility

_____ Want to see specialists without a referral

_____ Prescription costs

_____ Spouse/children/parent health care expenses

_____ Low copay/deductible/coinsurance

_____ Help with considerable out-of-pocket expenses

_____ Greater control over health care spending with decision-support tools

_____ Chronic disease

_____ Vision/dental (braces) costs

_____ Discounts for alternative health care such as vitamins, acupuncture, aromatherapy, massage therapy, wellness programs

Use this checklist as a guide to compare health plans and speak to your employer's benefits consultant about which options may be best for you.

For more information on options to consider, go to *www.planforyourhealth.com.*

Choosing the Right Health Plan Questionnaire

Benefits consultants are working with major insurers to develop more consumer-friendly Web sites to help employees choose plans, providers and services. One of the leading medical Web sites, WebMD, suggests you find three insurance plans that seem right for you and ask the following questions to help you determine which one best suits your needs.

- *Do members rate the plan highly on things that are important to us?*
- *Does the plan provide preventive services to help keep my family well?*
- *Does it do a good job of helping them get better when they are sick?*
- *Is the plan accredited?*
- *Does the plan have the doctors and hospitals I want or need?*
- *Does the plan provide the benefits I need?*
- *Do the doctors, pharmacies, and other services in the plan have convenient times and locations?*
- *Does the plan meet by budget?*

The answers to these questions may not be as simple as "yes" or "no." Still, these questions should help you to think about and compare your health plan choices.

*Life Insurance Worksheet**

EXPENSES

Surviving spouse's annual living expenses   _____

Years Needed   _____

Children's annual living expenses   _____

Years Needed   _____

Child Care   _____

Years Needed   _____

Funeral and estate settlement expenses   _____

Emergency fund   _____

Outstanding debts   _____

TOTAL NEEDED   _____

ASSETS   _____

Surviving spouse's after-tax income   _____

Yearly Social Security benefits   _____

Years until youngest child turns 16   _____

Current assets available   _____

Existing life insurance already owned   _____

TOTAL CURRENT INSURANCE   _____

TOTAL NEEDED   _____

ADDITIONAL INSURANCE NEEDED   _____

---

*Source: "How Much Life Insurance Do You need?" *SmartMoney.com.*

- - - - - - - - - - - - - -

Net Worth Worksheet
for Estate Plan

ASSETS

Value of home(s) (market value, not equity)   _____

Value of car(s)   _____

Value of other vehicles   _____

Jewelry   _____

Furniture   _____

Artwork   _____

Cameras, computers, other physical assets   _____

Checking and savings accounts   _____

CDs and savings bonds   _____

Brokerage accounts   _____

Retirement accounts (401(k)s, IRAs, pensions)   _____

Life insurance death benefit   _____

Other assets   _____

LIABILITIES

Mortgage balance   _____

Home equity loans   _____

Car loans   _____

College loans   _____

Other debts   _____

TOTAL NET WORTH   _____

INDEX